LIBERTY & JUSTICE
OF
ECONOMIC EQUILIBRIUM

Liberty & Justice
of
Economic Equilibrium

An Economic Justice Textbook

Justice of the Divine Economy

BRUCE KOERBER

OL26236311M

Dedicated to Shoghi Effendi (1897–1957),
the Guardian of the Bahá'í Faith

and

dedicated to Ludwig von Mises (1881–1973),
"the last knight of liberalism."

Contents

Foreword

The evolution of a society, including the evolution of its economic system, is closely linked to changes in the value system that underlies all its manifestations. The values a society lives by will determine its world view and religious institutions, its scientific enterprise and technology, and its political and economic arrangements. Once the collective set of values and goals has been expressed and codified, it will constitute the framework of the society's perceptions, insights, and choices for innovation and social adaptation. As the cultural value system changes—often in response to environmental challenges—new patterns of cultural evolution will emerge. [18, p. 197]   —Fritjof Capra

It is inevitable that we will have to commit to new ideas and embrace common goals as Fritjof Capra has passionately called for and described as a 'cultural evolution.' The world is in dire circumstances and a majority of the human race is poor, hungry, and destitute. The piecemeal attempts at putting our house in order are meagre and limited in scope. They lack the holistic approach needed in a world that we have convinced ourselves of becoming global, when in fact it is only global as far as the market is concerned. The so-called economic or financial crisis is neither economic nor financial. It is, above all, a crisis which is the result of greed, selfishness, and the absence of all forms of ethical and moral principles. At present, the problems and proposed solutions are linked to economics as never before. In recent decades, critics of the international economic system have also focused attention on important issues such as protecting the environment and upholding workers' rights. An integrated perspective therefore becomes necessary and important.

The recent revolution, which has ushered in the information age, is not without looming threats and dangers, as Ian Angell suggests in his book *The New Barbarian Manifesto: How to Survive the Information Age*. The book is a chilling portrait of a world in accelerated upheaval, prompted by the ramifications of information technology. He opens his introductory chapter by quoting Charles Dickens:

> It was the best of times, it was the worst of times, it was the age of wisdom, it was the age of foolishness, it was the epoch of belief, it was the epoch of incredulity, it was the season of Light, it was the season of Darkness, it was the spring of hope, it was the winter of despair, we had everything before us, we had nothing before us, we were all going direct to Heaven, we were all going direct the other way.[19, p. 1]

Fluidity may be the main characteristic of this "best of times" or the "worst of times." The uncertainty that Angell speaks of had already been expressed in these two lines of Matthew Arnold (1822–1888):

> Wandering between two worlds, one dead,
> The other powerless to be born.[10, p. 161]

The promised world "powerless to be born" seems to be hampered and restrained by the absence of that dynamic power of the spirit and the overwhelming dominance of materialist culture.

Debates on this subject of a world in upheaval, especially in policy-making circles, are often shaped by "the politics of time," as distinct from "the politics of eternity," and are purely concerned with national interests especially economic interests. Such interests, though, are parochial, whereas if the phenomenon of globalization were to be carefully examined, it would be recognised as being capable of creating an impact far beyond these narrow limitations, so that discussions of the subject should properly extend to encompass cultural and spiritual aspects.

If we are to have a lasting global society then we will need to adopt a holistic approach. Indeed, the most urgent question associated with globalization today is how to ensure that the dictates of universal *integration* be not at the cost of the *integrity* of the component parts.

Economics and communication technology have brought the peoples of this planet together, and they have made positive contributions; but they have not, and will not, create a peaceful world order by themselves. They have yet to overcome the inhibitions and resistance to change. At present there are several quite extreme theories of economics, none of which has proved to be a workable system that could be adopted internationally or found a way to alleviate the suffering of millions who are living in poverty. If the formula of economics combined with technology was viable in and of itself, the twentieth century would have been an age of peace rather than a long cycle of crises.

Globalization of our economies is in fact inevitable and highly profitable. The promise is that through these new international trading and economic processes, glibly labelled 'free trade', humanity will eventually enter a prosperous new era that will free it from war or deprivation and lead to far-reaching changes, which at once will establish the principle not only of free, but also of fair trade.

Mr. Bruce Koerber in his new book, *Liberty and Justice of Economic Equilibrium*, attempts to bring back to the world of economics those ethical values and spiritual moral principles which Edmund Burke, a century and a half ago, lamented their loss when he stated:

> The age of chivalry is gone. —That of sophisters, economists, and calculators, has succeeded; and the glory of Europe is extinguished forever. Never, never more, shall we behold a generous loyalty to rank and sex, that proud submission, that dignified obedience, that subordination of the heart, which kept alive, even in servitude itself, the spirit of an exalted freedom. The unbought grace of life, achieved defensive nations, the nurse of the manly sentiment and heroic enterprise is gone! It is gone, that sensibility of principle, that chastity of honor, which felt a stain like a wound, which inspired courage while it mitigated ferocity, which ennobled whatever it touched, and under which vice itself lost half its evil, by losing all its grossness. [17, pp. 515–516]

In *Liberty and Justice of Economic Equilibrium*, concepts such as economics and ethics, a divine economy, liberty and justice, and harmony and reciprocity are emphasized but the main inspiration behind the book is the principle of world order which Bahá'u'lláh (1817–1892) revealed to the world and was founded on three major principles: Justice, Unity, and Peace. This formula is irreversible for without justice, we cannot create unity and without unity, we can never create peace. Perhaps no other poet of modern times understood the concept of justice in our buying and selling than the Lebanese-American poet, Kahlil Gibran (1883–1931):

> To you the earth yields her fruit, and you shall not want if you but know how to fill your hands.
> It is in exchanging the gifts of the earth that you shall find abundance and be satisfied.
> Yet unless the exchange be in love and kindly justice, it will but lead some to greed and others to hunger...
> And before you leave the market place, see that no one has gone his way with empty hands.
> For the master spirit of the earth shall not sleep peacefully upon the wind till the needs of the least of you are satisfied.[24, pp. 100-101]

Suheil Bushrui, BA, PhD, Hon LHD

Research Professor Emeritus,
The University of Maryland

Professor and Director,
The George and Lisa Zakhem Kahlil Gibran Chair for Values and Peace

Senior Scholar (Peace Studies)
The Center for International Development and Conflict Management

List of Figures

Introduction

INCUBATION

Who are you? Who am I? We are products of our culture. But we are more than that and to this I will return. Culture influences us, all the way from the past and most definitely in the present while at the same time culture is influenced by us, laying the groundwork for the culture of the future. This reciprocity inherently exists, demonstrating the inseparability of the actions of individuals and the fruits of those actions. The fruits then go on to nourish and energize more action.

What we are talking about is human culture, that is, the nest created and originating from the logical structure of human thought, a structure which is universally shared by all people. To quote Ludwig von Mises: "The logical structure of human thought is immutable throughout the whole course of time and is the same for all races, nations, and classes."[49, p. 217] Despite our diversity we are essentially in unity as humans—one species—who are, gradually over time, discovering the richness of our potential as contributors to this very beautiful and unfolding culture.

We've come a long way: "The life of primitive man was an unceasing struggle against the scantiness of the nature-given means for sustenance. In this desperate effort to secure bare survival, many individuals and whole families, tribes, and races succumbed. Primitive man was always haunted by the specter of death from starvation. Civilization has freed us from these perils."[48, p. 602] One of the reasons that

Liberty   Justice

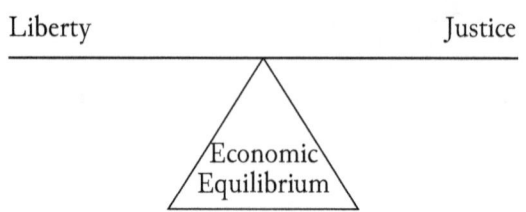

Diagram I1: The Liberty and Justice of Economic Equilibrium

humankind is no longer primitive is because of the increased flow of knowledge due to the development of language, which facilitated the search for truth, and it is this keenness of vision that enhances the keenness of understanding. Consequently, "Men always strive for an improvement in their conditions and always will. This is man's inescapable destiny."[46, p. 190]

As a testimony of the aforementioned logical structure of thought I have chosen a pattern to use as I unfold the storyline in this book on liberty and justice. It follows a sequence that will be present in each chapter and throughout this book. And so, early on, each theme will show evidence of a process of incubation highlighting its development but at some transition point it matures enough to offer shelter as a tabernacle and even to move around and become a mobile factor in society. Its culmination comes about when it can either be critically examined and tested itself, or when it can be the instrument used for testing by the assayer.

With regards testing, "What makes natural science possible is the power to experiment; what makes social science possible is the power to grasp or to comprehend the meaning of human action."[47, p. 9] Using the deductive or a priori method to bridge the gaps between the world of things and the world of thoughts and emotions—and reasoning from previous experience or from established principles to particular facts—we proceed, confirming observation and experimental data as a well as replacing them. Such is life on the cutting edge!

TABERNACLE

We are more than our cultural influences. We are each unique, and mostly unpolished gems, yet the degree and type of polishing is strongly determined by the influence of culture. If our inherent dual nature is kept a secret from us by these cultural influences then we are more likely to fall victim to the promoters of half-truths. Or if the side of our gem that is attached to the earth is the side that is polished our ego makes it appear to us that we need to be victors over others. Ideally though; our potentials will shine as a result of cultural influences that polish the heaven-facing side of the gem so that: our love of self is justly a recognition of our subjective nature, and we understand that social cooperation is what benefits each and all of us the most.

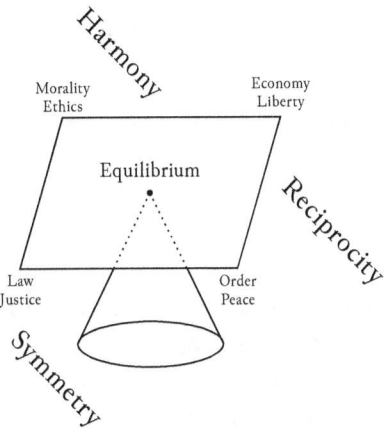

Diagram I2: Human Civilization Equilibrium

This inseparability between the individual and the surrounding culture is part of the symmetry and harmony and reciprocity exhibited throughout all of what we think to be reality. For instance, there is inseparability between micro and macro economics (likewise between atoms and the universe) and between economics and ethics. There is inseparability between liberty and justice and likewise between law and order.

If connected—then by what force—and how does this force operate? Gravity causes a pendulum to swing from a high point to the lowest point until it comes to rest. Similarly the force of equilibrium brings all things towards harmony. It can be symbolized by a circle as in Diagram I3, where this force of harmony is seen as all-pervading. And since the circle is used to symbolize equilibrium it can be said to represent potentials known as omniscience, omnipresence, and omnipotence. It is this circle, then, that is given the designation 'divine economy' [34, p. 13] because it represents a new definition of equilibrium, the definition of equilibrium used in the divine economy theory.

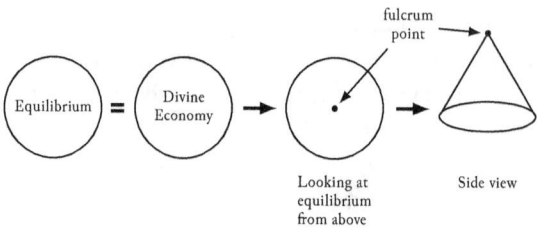

Diagram 13: Equilibrium Perspectives

ASSAY

It may be that some will misunderstand divine economy theory from their very first introduction to it simply because the word 'divine' causes certain incorrect associations to come to mind. The all-pervasive, all-compelling force of harmony that is behind all equilibrating tendencies is divine; simply because it is beyond human comprehension.

Consider an analogy with yogurt. If active starter is added to some milk then universal fermentation begins and culture forms. For the substrate of human civilization the natural starters are economics, ethics, liberty (order), and justice (law). These are what create the culture of an ever-advancing civilization. Contamination by any agent that creates disharmony pollutes the culture, rendering it putrid.

Look around and see if there is evidence that the human culture has been contaminated. It is easy to see that we are at a critical point in history. Left alone—without the benefits of state-of-the-art knowledge of economics, ethics, liberty and justice—the culture will continue to spoil. But that is not what we are going to do. Instead our objective is to explore the error-plagued systems, to raise everyone's awareness of state-of-the-art science, and thereby provide the necessary tools to evaluate and correct the errors. "It is vain to object that life and reality are not logical. Life and reality are neither logical nor illogical; they are simply given. But logic is the only tool available to man for the comprehension of both."[48, p. 67]

What seems to have escaped analysts in the past is the power of economic equilibrium as the fulcrum that brings into perfect balance law and order and ultimately liberty and justice. Perhaps Mises puts his finger on it best: "The economist must never be a specialist. In dealing with any problem he must always fix his glance upon the whole system."[25, p. 157] In this book we are about to embark on a training to be an assayer with the ability to detect impurities and corruption, to intimately understand the substrate of human civilization, to identify those elements that add value, and to ultimately declare what it is that brings about wealth.

Chapter 1
In Need Of Healing

Economics and Ethics
& Law and Order—To Date

Preamble

It is an eye opening experience, even if entered upon reluctantly, to be
thrust into a world that is locked in its ways—hypocritical to its core.
This is the perspective of adolescents when they find themselves at the
threshold of adulthood. How ridiculous; to blindly adhere to practices
that are obviously unjust. Exasperated, they exclaim: "These people know
absolutely nothing!"

Incubation

It is a formidable task to describe the status of human civilization to
date with mere words and in a single chapter, nevertheless that is my
task. I have chosen as a starting point and as a reference point a 'modern
city' in the period of history known as the High Middle Ages (between
the 11th century and the end of the 13th century). What is significant
about this city is that it was located in Europe which means that it was
under the cultural influence of Christianity. The principal underlying
ethic that set social boundaries was "Render therefore unto Caesar the
things which be Caesar's, and unto God the things which be God's."[38]

Such a 'modern city' in those days was a place of peace and commerce. People were guided in their relationships with each other by
the teachings of Christianity and property rights were protected from
unwarranted confiscation, which led to the accumulation of capital, and

it was property rights and capital accumulation and unobtrusive law that were the catalysts for the advancement of Western civilization.

There was no manmade law. "Law was conceived of, not as something enacted (legislated), but as something existing, which it was necessary to discover."[37, p. 141] When necessary, nobles were assigned the task of determining what was right in the context of eternal law.

Of course not all cities, even in the culture of what can be called Western civilization, were equally enlightened nor did these modern cities with a higher degree of righteousness remain uncorrupted over time. Asymmetry crept in and reciprocity waned.

Power-to-be-had was enticing. The dual nature of human beings cannot be forgotten as a factor in history since there can be no doubt that it played a significant role in the history of human civilization. Let us assume that one person becomes ego-driven and lusts after power. That affects history. But it is not just one person lusting after power, it is many. And because humans are all connected within society and within civilization, all are affected by this.

How is civilization affected? All things associated with human thought and activity feel the effects. This means that economics and ethics, and justice and liberty, and law and order, and peace and prosperity are all changed in a negative way. Also, consequently, what is considered as education is altered. The disconnection caused by the exercising of the lower human nature reverberates and is amplified and compounded. It is not necessarily a condition of chaos but it is disorder, and it is destructive.

One of the first wounds inflicted, always, is the loss of property rights (which are essentially human rights). Arbitrariness takes the place of mutuality. The system of mutual gain from social cooperation morphs into a system where some people benefit at the expense of others, all of which is the outcome of the arbitrariness of ego-driven interventionism. In other words, no longer does everyone have equal freedom to make choices. "No doubt there is no liberty when people cannot do all that the laws allow them to do; but laws could forbid so many things as to abolish liberty altogether."[37, p. 152] The deprivation of freedom then also weakens the moral fiber of the people in society, the fiber that is necessary to repel the furtherance of injustice.

TABERNACLE

What we are then witnessing is the seed of the destruction of civilization. This is the trend towards no ethics, no justice, and no liberty. It can be traced back to the use of power to take advantage of others. It starts with an individual but it expands. This is the beginning of State formation! There are only two ways to acquire property and wealth: through production (economic means) or through coercive expropriation (political means).

As it expands it creates a political class. The incentives within such an environment stimulates even more ego-driven ambition to intervene in more and more ways, expanding in all directions with the far-off ultimate goal to gain complete monopoly control, with the power to confiscate and distribute without restraint.

As the State becomes a pervasive influence in the culture it begins to control the information about itself and begins to weave myths about its merits. It finds ways to bring within the confines of its tabernacle the representatives of science and religion and uses these 'tools' to do two things: 1) to reduce opposition from people who depend on these authority figures for their judgments, 2) to create a culture of relative morality, weakening both science and religion in everyone's eyes, thereby weakening any opposition by leaders of science and religion as the potential rivals to the absolute State.

Also brought within its tabernacle are the other social institutions for the purpose of increasing its power. What we have are economics professionals and legal professionals including legislators and politicians all serving to promote the goals of the State. This is the point where the political class that benefits from the wealth transfer theory of government becomes the new aristocracy with separate, special 'legal' interests. "Whoever wields law has power over everyone else."[28, pp. 68–69]

At this point the State has succeeded in altering the perception of law: as something that is made by the government. The morphing of common law into authoritarian law creates with it authoritarian rights which imply restrictions on private property and individual rights and subsequent involuntary transfers. The State and self-interested lawyers benefit from this non-codified, authoritarian law.

Law decreed by legislation is at variance with the market process. Rather than free exchanges the exchange process is coerced. In a free market all coercive extraction of wealth is considered to be robbery and the perpetrator is considered a thief.

Monopoly powers in law and in judicial services necessarily leads to overproduction of these services and overcharging for them. For example, "once a judicial monopoly has been established, its agents— the government—also become and will naturally strive to expand their role as judge and arbitrator of last resort in all family matters."[52, pp. 1–8, 110–117] Unlike a private insurance company, if the State fails to prevent crime there is no indemnity. And since there is no indemnity the State has no more incentive to solve the crime than to just file it away as a recorded event. The incentive, as a monopolist with coercive power, is simply to demand more resources. If a criminal is found there is no restitution but rather the cost of caring for the criminal is passed along to the victim as a tax. "The adversarial nature of authoritarian law pits group against group in the taking/transfer process and promotes disorder rather than order."[16, p. 77]

What recourse is there? The State is a monopolistic judicial system at the various and different levels but never are these independent— rather—there always is a vested interest in expanding the power and dominion of the State. For instance, "Judges are appointed or elected for long terms, up to life, and they are accorded a monopoly of decision-making in their particular area."[54, p. 240] The incentive for public judges is to choose easy cases, not the ones that produce precedents. Therefore there is little or no refinement of property rights.

As a result there is nothing to prevent the State from penetrating deeper and deeper into the economy. For example, "There is no tenable economic, legal, moral, or spiritual rationale that could be adduced in justification of paper money and fractional-reserve banking. The prevailing ways of money production, relying as they do on a panoply of legal privileges, are alien elements in the capitalist [i.e., true free market] economy. They provide illicit incomes, encourage irresponsibility and dependence, stimulate the artificial centralization of political and economic decision-making, and constantly create fundamental disequilibria that threaten the life and welfare of millions of people."[31, pp. 238–239]

The aspiring for power by the State is eliminative. Lesser entities are gobbled up and centralization increases even despite the so-called 'checks and balances.' Take for an example the States rights conferred in the United States Constitution. The expansive U.S. federal government has almost completely usurped all of the States rights. Almost gone is that check and balance at the time of this writing. The order, or more accurately, the disorder that will in the end come from this eliminative centralization is totalitarianism and tyrannical rule.

Let us again consider the monopoly power of the State. Those things that for an individual are deemed as crimes are deemed as legal for the State. To coercively take the property of another is acceptable if the State is the aggressor. To fraudulently multiply the money stock as a way to extract wealth from people in the community is called counterfeiting and it is a crime unless it is done by the State. Now consider the regulations and laws that are touted to offer protection against the evils of monopoly power. Yet the State is a gigantic conglomeration of a growing number of monopolies. Where is the 'anti-trust' fervor against these monopolies? The monopoly control of the legal system rules that out!

Assay

To further understand the pervasive disorder let us take a look at the status of the fulcrum. The equilibrium force is being assaulted from all directions, causing disharmony, asymmetry, and imbalance. With the equilibrium force undermined by human intervention into and against the economy we also find that the ethics and law of the natural order are corrupted, and liberty and justice are trampled upon, and peace and prosperity are assaulted. To those who talk about a 'mixed economy' there is no such thing that is sustainable in the long run simply because interventionism is unnatural, immoral, and unjust.

There are only two reasons why the State is able to sustain itself. It has the power of coercion which indirectly includes the power of the belief of those who are being ruled; that State power is needed for law and order to exist. The second reason is the inefficiency of the State agents! "But for the inefficiency of the law-givers and the laxity, carelessness, and corruption of many of the functionaries, the last vestiges of the market economy would have long since disappeared." [48, p. 859] If the State agencies or the State agents could overcome their inherently and characteristically lethargic and inept bureaucratic quagmire then people would more quickly see the emergence of the totalitarian State—and alarmed—they would revolt against it.

Rest assured, the State is not a natural order and this can be easily proven by the divine economy theory. All ego-driven intervention disrupts equilibrium. The State is the best means only if the ends desired is despotism. "The main political problem is how to prevent the rulers from becoming despots and enslaving the citizenry."[40, p. 454] Without the State the natural order of social cooperation would prevail. "The State is the only institution entitled to apply coercion and compulsion and to inflict harm upon individuals. This tremendous power cannot be abandoned to the discretion of some men, however competent and clever they may deem themselves. It is necessary to restrict its application. This is the task of the laws."[44, p. 76] Summarily it is these laws that are compatible with liberty and justice and these are the laws that we are interested in exploring.

Selected Exercises

1. What were the catalysts for the advancement of Western Civilization??

2. Describe the beginning of State formation.

3. What process moves the State towards totalitarianism?

Chapter 2
But Left Dangling

Unfolding Law and Order

But really, deep down inside, there is very little confidence in adolescence. How could there be? Experience is limited, knowledge is barely acquired with little or no time for contemplation; and so wisdom is in short supply. Are the surrounding hypocrisies readily witnessed just a way of life? Maybe what appears ridiculous is really all the best we can do or expect to do. Wondering and pondering: "Am I stuck in the mud, doomed to slowly sink into it?"

INCUBATION

What we have is a need to translate that which is subjective into something that is objective. Justice is the step taken to objectify the ethics that protects the subjective qualities of human action. The challenge is to have the origin of this step come from a realm that is itself wholly objective or 'blind' of all vested interests.

Justice is a known concept because it is either present or absent and therefore it is able to be perceived. It exists in the context of human relationships and human civilization. That which promotes social cooperation among everyone in the long run is just. Immediately we see the difficulty of discovering the forever elusive absolute justice and realize that we must fall back to a lesser position of relative justice, that is, justice that is appropriate for the epoch of human history we are living in. But no matter which epoch, "Conduct suited to preserve social cooperation is just, conduct detrimental to the preservation of society is unjust."[45, p. 54]

Because justice is natural and part of human society it is perceivable. The reason it is natural is simply because social cooperation is the normal pattern within human society. Very early on human beings discovered the value of cooperation and chose it instead of isolation. This choice led to advancement and yet at the same time it created a system of social values that constituted a more complex and more satisfying practice. Through these voluntary interactions, which included service to others, society came into existence, not as an entity in itself but as a product of social cooperation.

It turned out that this cooperation was a way to optimize productive non-violent human energy. "It is obvious that social cooperation would not have evolved and could not be preserved if the immense majority were not to consider it as the means for the attainment of all their ends."[45, p. 51] There has always been a tremendous amount of empirical data in the form of historical records documenting the success of economic cooperation. The choices available with cooperation were greater. People cooperating were able to make gains (profits) psychically and in material well-being. Agreements were part of this voluntary process and they naturally became contractual[1], in a real sense.

Balance among all of these interactions was recognized and it was also discovered that the present and the future of society were brought into balance by savings and the use of capital. This tendency towards some kind of equilibrium over time began to be understood.

This discernment and alertness that is characteristic of human beings is the first step in the truth-seeking process: "Truth-seeking is a means to an end, as ethics is a means to an end. And the end is to substitute a more satisfactory state of affairs for a less satisfactory state."[26, p. 239] What then kicks in is logic and the use of reason to devise a method to gain greater understanding. "One method applicable to almost all problems is what we may call either the *deductive* or the *a priori* method. This method reaches a conclusion without observation or experiment. It consists in reasoning from previous experience or from

---

1. "Contract law as the 'law' that parties themselves bring into existence by their agreement—the transition from customary law to contract law becomes a very easy one indeed." See reference [23, p. 224].

established principles to particular facts. It may, however, be used to confirm observation and experiment as well as to take their place."[27, p. 20]

But don't forget that the signs of prosperity can and do attract the attention of the ego-driven. To interpose oneself without consequent penalties would be the most preferred situation for the ego-driven, hence we can see why attempts to structure laws in an artificial way can come under the influence of anti-social (someone who weakens or destroys the natural processes in society) individuals.

Concurrently, as part of the natural processes taking place in society, the practice of good manners facilitates social cooperation and so these manners become the norms that constitute the morality of the society. Those who practice this morality are supportive of the society, recognize the wisdom of ethics, and are likely to succeed. "There is hardly an ethical problem, in fact, without its economic aspect. Our daily ethical decisions are in the main economic decisions, and nearly all our daily economic decisions have, in turn, an ethical aspect."[26, p. 301]

To go against the norms, to act immorally, and to run counter to the wisdom of ethics requires two things: an ego-driven motivation, and an economic incentive. Law can either eliminate that incentive or enable it. "Law tended to become secular and independent of theology sooner than did ethics. It also became more definite and explicit."[26, p. 64] The misunderstanding of the source of law and the misuse of law, thus, has negative consequences.

Laws exist all around us. The natural world throughout the expansive universe operates according to laws. As long as humans sought greater understanding of things the approach has always been to discover the laws. The same attitude was adopted for millennia in order to try to grasp how individuals are to behave in society. "Furthermore, classical jurists never entertained pretensions of being 'original' or 'clever,' but rather were 'the servants of certain fundamental principles, and as Savigny pointed out, herein lies their greatness.' Their fundamental objective was to discover the universal principles of law, which are unchanging and inherent in the logic of human relationships. It is true, however, that social evolution itself often necessitates the application of these unchanging universal principles to new situations and problems arising continually from this evolutionary process."[29, pp. 24–25]

Of course religion played a prominent role in the development of law in the Western civilization.

It was through this objectifying process that norms were formalized into laws and it was through this process that formalized procedures of how to deal with new circumstances were deduced. This formalization is itself natural: there is a definite advantage to society when uncertainty decreases and certainty increases. Laws in this sense do just that, especially when they are discovered (rather than created arbitrarily). Properly formalized, with the discovery process kept intact, laws define rights.

From the religious point of view—half-baked in the oven of Western civilization—moral values and ethics were viewed as absolute. Yet at the same time economic values attributed to things by people were and are necessarily subjective. It is the purpose of law to objectify these in a harmonious way. "Moral judgments do have objective binding force on the individual. And moral rules are objective not only in the sense that they call for objective actions but that they call for objective adherence by everybody."[26, p. 168] "As voluntary economic cooperation makes us more interdependent, the consequences of breaches of cooperation or a breakdown of the system become more serious for all of us; and to the extent that we recognize this we will become less indifferent to failure or violation of cooperation in ourselves or in others. Therefore the tendency will be for the moral level of the whole community to be kept high or to be raised."[26, p. 323]

Rights, that is rights formalized by law, describe what 'belongs' to a human being. Considering that God created human beings 'in His Image' the rights belonging to him and her are sacred. Since these are natural it should be evident exactly what it is that laws protect. In accordance with the ethics of social cooperation and the exalted station bestowed on humans by God, liberty is a principal right. Humans love freedom. Property rights are human rights and once these are granted the economy has the foundation it needs to perpetuate social cooperation. "Social cooperation, however, can be based only on the foundation of private ownership of the means of production."[49, p. 40]

It is law that protects property rights that are so essential to freedom. "All production, all civilization, rests on recognition of and respect for property rights. A free enterprise system is impossible without security of property as well as security of life. Free enterprise is possible only within a framework of law and order and morality. This means that free enterprise presupposes morality; but, as we shall later see, it also helps to preserve and promote it."[26, p. 303] Freedom from the State is what made the political anarchy of Western civilization, which operated according to the principles of classical liberalism, so prosperous relatively speaking. "If history could teach us anything, it would be that private property is inextricably linked with civilization."[51, p. 58]

TABERNACLE

How does all of this fit together within a perfectly balanced and harmonized and symmetrical plane of existence? I know it is not realistic to assume that all these phenomena of such immense complexity could fit into a single plane. But it is exactly because of the complexity that a simple model can be useful and can assist us in gaining a greater understanding.

First of all, and this is a moot point, the model I am about to use is not two dimensional like a plane but rather it is three dimensional. Imagine a fulcrum that is positioned under a two dimensional plane. The tip of the fulcrum is at the center so that the plane is balanced perfectly. It is this balanced state of affairs that we will call equilibrium.

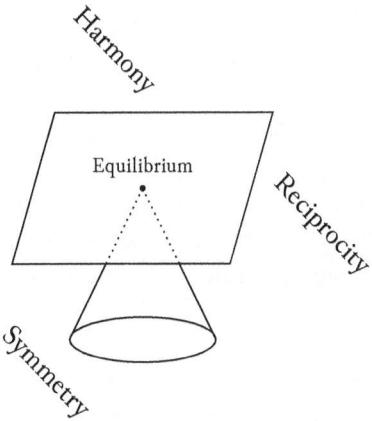

Diagram 2a: Economic Equilibrium and the Forces at Work

In its simplest representation, shown in Diagram 2a, we see the plane at rest in its equilibrium position. We also see the forces that help to maintain the equilibrium: harmony, reciprocity and symmetry. In Diagram 2b the immense complexities that come into play in human culture are added to provide a picture of the interconnectedness of all facets of human civilization.

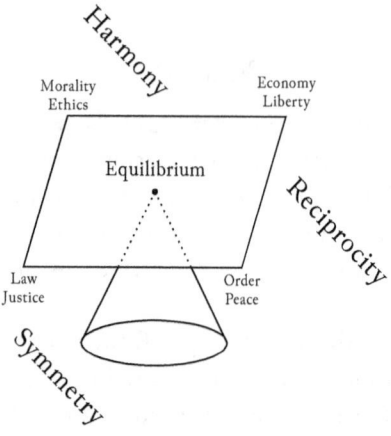

Diagram 2b: Human Civilization Equilibrium

Ponder: "'In ethics a common ground for the choice of rules of conduct is given so far as people agree in considering the preservation of social cooperation the foremost means for attaining all their ends.' Now if we adopt this explanation, we recognize that Justice is not the ultimate ethical end, existing purely for its own sake, but is primarily a means, and even a means to a means. Justice and Freedom are the great means to the promotion of Social Cooperation, which in turn is the great means to the realization of each individual's ends and therefore to the realization of the ends of 'society.' The subordination of Justice to a 'mere' means, however important that means is regarded to be, may come as a shock to many moral philosophers, who have been accustomed to regard it as the supreme ethical end... Justice was made for man, not man for justice."[26, pp. 255–256] And ponder: "That justice is primarily a means to social cooperation, that social cooperation is primarily a means to promote the maximum happiness and well-being of each and all, does not reduce the importance of either justice or social cooperation. For both are the necessary means, the indispensable means to the desired goal. And therefore both of them are to be valued and cherished as ends-in-themselves. For a means can also be an end, if not the ultimate end. It can even seem to form an integral part of the ultimate end. The happiness and well being of men simply cannot be achieved, and hardly imagined, without Justice and Social Cooperation."[26, pp. 259–260]

Now with this in mind try to imagine what the effect would be if something would come into the picture and distort the natural reciprocity that occurs as a part of social cooperation. For example, if the mutually agreed upon terms of a contract were altered by an act of intervention then not only is the agreed upon reciprocity altered but it causes disharmony and other kinds of asymmetries. It's funny. It is popular knowledge that there are consequences resulting from disruptions of the ecological system even to the extent that the flapping of a butterfly wing is felt all around the world, and yet there is little thought given to the consequences of the major and continuous human disruptions to the equilibrium that is operative in human civilization!

Another interesting feature of the Human Civilization Equilibrium diagram is the listing of eight means/ends arranged at the corners of the plane. As addressed by many authors and as addressed by me in *Ethical Economics for Today and Tomorrow...*, part of the reason ethics and economics are inseparable is because of the interchangeability of the ends and means depending on the particular circumstances. Even this fogginess is cleared up considerably, although not completely, by this diagram. According to the diagram, the strongest of 'ends' is equilibrium. The next strongest 'ends' are harmony and reciprocity and symmetry even though they also have strong 'means' characteristics.

It is true that equilibrium is highly regarded as an ends but it is more accurate to regard it as the force that always drives society towards the ultimate end. The ultimate end for humans, since we are social beings in addition to our reality as spiritual beings, is social cooperation. "As social cooperation is the great means of achieving nearly all our individual ends, this means can be thought of as itself the moral goal to be achieved."[26, p. xi] With this in mind re-examine the Human Civilization Equilibrium diagram and notice how all of the means: Harmony/Reciprocity/Symmetry; plus Morality/Ethics, Economy/Liberty, Law/Justice, and Order/Peace, serve to bring about and fortify social cooperation as driven by the force of equilibrium.

"Though liberty is beyond doubt an end-in-itself, it is also of the highest value, to repeat, as a means to most of our other ends. We can pursue not only our economic but our intellectual and spiritual goals only if we are free to do so. Only when we are free do we have the power to choose. And only when we have the power to choose can our choice be called right or moral."[26, pp. 267–268] Remember the title of this book and how it is portrayed as a simple two dimensional figure balancing liberty and justice on either end of a fulcrum. (Diagram I₁ on Page 2) That is a simpler representation, a shorthand version, of the Human Civilization Equilibrium diagram. As food for thought ponder this: that just like liberty and justice can be imagined as being in equilibrium so can we imagine, balanced across a fulcrum, their counterparts—Economy and Law (Diagram 2c).

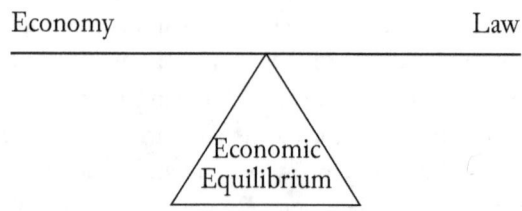

Diagram 2c: Economy and Law in Equilibrium

Surely the economy is intimately connected to law. Now consider the implications of law and justice being harmonious and symmetrical, and emanating reciprocity optimally in a natural equilibrium environment as shown in Diagram 2d. Justice is present or injustice is present, depending on whether law is natural or whether its derivation is ego-driven.

Here is an additional point of contemplation. Equilibrium is not instantaneous, it is a tendency and if it is achieved it happens in the future. In other words, the Human Civilization Equilibrium diagram has another dimension that is implied. The time element is necessarily a part of the long-run nature of equilibrium. "We have seen that there tends to be a *coincidence* between the actions or rules of action that best

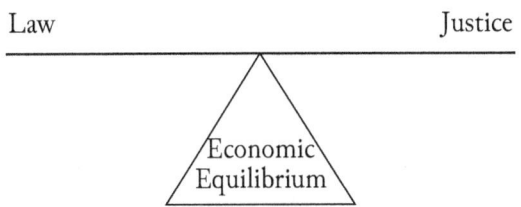

Diagram 2d: Law and Justice in Equilibrium

promote the interests of the individual in the long run and the rules of action that best promote the interests of society as a whole in the long run. We have seen that this coincidence tends to be greater the longer the period we take into consideration."[26, p. 108]

ASSAY

In Chapter 1 we saw why human civilization has its current pattern. However it would be mistaken to think that the impetus behind the changes that have historically taken place is a negative one. It is still the force of equilibrium at work but sadly it kept getting altered and distorted along the way. "For example, the entire law merchant was developed, not by the State or in State courts, but by private merchant courts. It was only much later that government took over mercantile law from its development in merchants' courts. The same occurred with admiralty law, the entire structure of the law of the sea, shipping, salvages, etc. Here again, the State was not interested, and its jurisdiction did not apply to the high seas; so the shippers themselves took on the task of not only applying, but working out the whole structure of admiralty law in their own private courts. Again, it was only later that the government appropriated admiralty law into its own courts."[54, p. 283]

What this suggests is that some of the cultural changes and some of the elements of civilization across the spectrum of history can be re-garded as natural. It is the classical liberalism perspective that serves as a guide to find these elements. "Customary law reflects the norms of those who choose to function in the particular social order 'governed' by those laws. In a very real sense, then, such customary law is a unanimously adopted 'social contract' or 'constitution.' It establishes the rules that are the basis for spontaneous social order. This social contract evolves and adapts to changing social conditions."[16, p. 322] "Because the source of recognition of customary law is reciprocity, private property rights and the rights of individual are likely to constitute the most important primary rules of conduct in such legal systems."[16, p. 13]

Human intelligence was behind the recognition that laws were in operation all around. As part of the search for a greater understanding of the laws certain individuals were seen as possessing more wisdom than others. Since humans are social beings it was understood that social cooperation was always the best environment and so the wise were sought out to help resolve disputes.

These were the nobles and the judges who served voluntarily in this capacity for the betterment of all. As circumstances changed over time these chosen wise ones studied how resolution was achieved in the past—and then within the context of eternal laws—strove to refine the law accordingly.

A major deterrent to breaking the law was avoidance of the consequence of social isolation resulting from ostracism. It was exactly because everyone recognized the noble or judge as wise and uncorrupt that the laws were abided by with unanimity. Another major deterrent has always been reward and punishment. "Justice hath a mighty force at its command. It is none other than reward and punishment for the deeds of men. By the power of this force the tabernacle of order is established throughout the world, causing the wicked to restrain their natures for fear of punishment."[13, p. 164]

Since laws were discovered within the context of the morality and unfolding ethics of the culture they were a part of the customs. A significant part of these customary laws pertained to exchanges between people within and also outside of their particular society and so the laws had the tendency towards being universally practiced. The best example is the Merchant's Law[2] which still is the foundation of international commerce today.

Part of the modernization of law was its formalization. Broadly speaking the legal code evolved into two basic forms: as codified

---

2. "By the end of the eleventh century, the Law Merchant had developed to such a degree that it governed virtually every aspect of commercial transactions in all of Europe." See reference [16, p. 31].

customary law and as common law. Codified law spelled it all out and it was therefore accessible to anyone who was interested. With common law "judges both made law and applied it. But common law had the defect of a wide margin of uncertainty."[26, p. 65] Common law eventually became the privileged arena of judges and lawyers. Obviously, restricted access and specialized jargon and legalistic methods created an enhanced opportunity for intervention. "Customary law and its institutions facilitate voluntary interactions; government law and its institutions facilitate involuntary transfers."[16, p. 101]

We have what appears to be two alternative scenarios. Diagram 2e shows the tabernacle of liberty and justice in place but it is barely able to protect the freedom of spirit from the burden of oppression from man-made laws. "Freedom in the moral sense does not mean freedom from causation, but freedom from compulsion."[26, p. 277] "Thus we may define freedom as that state of affairs in which the individual's discretion to choose is not constrained by governmental violence beyond the margin within which the praxeological law restricts it anyway."[30, p. 1023]

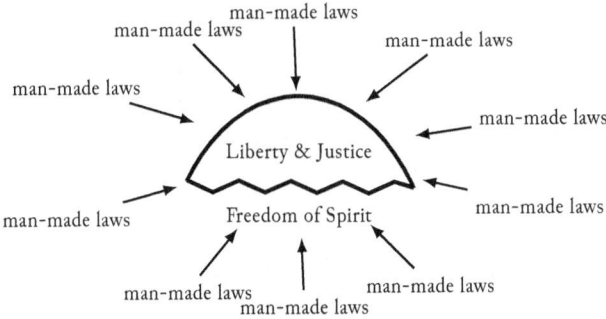

Diagram 2e: The Tabernacle of Liberty and Justice Bombarded by the Oppressiveness of Man-Made Laws

Diagram 2f is more hopeful. It shows justice and liberty as a strong and generous tabernacle sheltering the freedom of spirit from the precipitation from limited government. As we stated, laws are natural and can be discovered—rendering justice—and thereby optimizing social cooperation. "Justice is not purely as an end in itself. It is not

Limited Government

Freedom of Spirit

Diagram 2f: The Tabernacle of Liberty and Justice Protects the Freedom of Spirit from Limited Government

an ideal that can be isolated from its consequences. Though admittedly an intermediate end, it is primarily a means. Justice, in brief, consists of the social arrangements and rules that are most conducive to social cooperation—which means, in the economic field, most conducive to maximizing production. And the justice of these arrangements and rules, in turn, is not to be judged purely by their effect in this or that isolated instance, but (in accordance with the principle first pointed out by Hume) by their over-all effect in the long run."[26, p. 317]

That is why understanding equilibrium as a divine force is so important. The resulting confidence will assure vigilant protection from the misdirected efforts of the ego-driven. The best and most effective way to apply this knowledge is to implement it at the correct scale—locally for instance—where the wisdom of certain individuals merits the confidence of others. Part of the trust in human civilization equilibrium is confidence that humans are truly one species, with the same logical structure of thought. What we will find is that these smaller scale societies will basically discover and practice laws which are perfectly compatible within human civilization as a whole. Although this societal diversity is nothing but political anarchy it has none of the negative biases associated with that term.

We seem to forget that we are traversing time and that ethical progress is a part of that journey. At this point in time we know some things with certainty. The natural and ethical basis of the economy is property rights and one of its corollaries—sound money. Another natural progression, known, that can function properly in a human civilization is federalism and its reciprocal—subsidiarity.

Practical law is no different than any other good or service. It is sought and it is provided. Those who provide it in a trustworthy way as an arbiter, or as a judge, or as a lawyer will be chosen and those who do not will not be chosen. Natural competition in a free market provides the necessary and real checks and balances against those who are ego-driven.

Can we visualize an alternative to the status quo of Statist law? "It is often difficult to see the important role customary law plays in determining the social order, since so much of custom has been codified or co-opted by common law courts and claimed as state law."[16, p. 228] The remnants of customary law still do exist and need to be strengthened. "Privatization in law and order involves two separate processes: 1) Increases in the privately owned and allocated resources devoted to the protection of persons and property, including the establishment and clarification of property rights through rule-making and adjudication; and 2) decreases in publicly controlled resources devoted to the same purposes."[16, p. 331]

The best way to get a feel for a modern set-up of a society based on private property is to refer to the writings and the audio and video recordings of Hans-Hermann Hoppe, a great economic scholar of the Austrian school of thought. Such a society is composed of three institutional devices, all of which currently exist. These three are: commercial insurance, freely financed judging agencies, and freely financed police forces. These can exist independently with a contractual alignment or they can exist as part of vertically integrated firms.

The "Rule of law, in the classical sense of the expression, cannot be maintained without actually securing the certainty of law, conceived as the possibility of long-run planning on the part of individuals in regards to their behavior in private life and business."[37, p. 95] It will be competing insurance companies that provide the major impetus for the development of a unified standard of law. Non-uniform standards would be culled because of their immeasurability, and arbitrary rules would be eliminated. As a result, uncertainty will be progressively removed and that new-found assurance and stability will attract clientele. The very real pressure to practice a defensible behavioral code—to not be an aggressor against the social norms—in order to be able to get and to be able to afford insurance will moderate people's behavior. Yet, diversified interests and risk profiles can still easily be provided for by insurance companies, simply by them designing specialized contracts.

Without doubt everyone in society has an interest in the development of a set of laws regarded as acceptable to everyone. Mutually agreed upon arbiters will settle disputes most easily. If the parties involved use different arbiters then an independent 3rd party arbiter will need to be chosen. And since all of the independent arbitration agencies are competing for clientele they have a very real incentive to gain a reputation for justice. It is then through this process of competition that a refined and unified law structure develops, one that increasingly—by its merits—becomes valid throughout the world. This is a part of the great process of economic and social integration which binds societies together despite the minor variations occurring within their internal law structures. This is the natural order of the modern world which is based on the property rights of individuals but which has been knocked off its path by the State.

Natural competition in a free market provides the necessary and real checks and balances for protection services and also for rehabilitation services for criminals. Certainly insurance companies will protect themselves and their clients by providing effective and productive protective services. Those that do it well will get more clients.

In a natural order mechanisms will develop that defend us from asocial individuals. Without a doubt laws are necessary for a society to survive. From day one the origin of human conflict resulted from some kind of a violation of property rights/human rights. "The purpose of law is to facilitate interaction and minimize conflict, three functions or branches of law are important: 1) determining individuals' property holdings (property law); 2) governing cooperative exchanges of property (contract law, including conveyancing); and 3) protecting persons and their property, including methods of property transfer, from third-party aggression (tort law)."[16, p. 351] The "private security market will be organized much like a mutual insurance market."[16, p. 359] Under these arrangements a firm or cooperative surety group organization insures individuals and their property against violations. The firm or organization, therefore, would have strong incentives to prevent offences by supplying police services with an emphasis on patrolling, watching, and other deterrents.

Rehabilitation of criminals due to their asocial behavior begins and ends with restitution to the victim. Victims of crimes will be fully compensated by criminals who will learn skills while they are producing marketable goods and services under a condition of restricted liberty. "Punishment will typically take the form of a 'fine' payable to the victim of at least sufficient magnitude to compensate the victim for all losses and cover the full cost of bringing the offender to justice. Although primary, fines may not be the only type of punishment."[16, p. 352] The opprobrium of the entire community may be a necessary additional step.

A convicted criminal can protect himself or herself from the most obvious abuses by having the choice of accepting bids for his services. "Because a prisoner's effort is directly rewarded, he can predict and partially determine the length of his prison term. Prisoner morale would improve, making eventual rehabilitation easier. There are a number of reasons to expect rehabilitation to be far more effective under such a system than it is with current efforts."[16, p. 369]

Obviously it can be said that we are not there yet. Some of the progress made to date has been camouflaged by the disarray caused by those who have disrupted the force of equilibrium. Stepping back and looking at human history we can see the tendency toward an ever-advancing civilization. If allowed to operate unhampered the equilibrium force that works by all of the various means within human civilization will bring peace and order. Besides, there is no moral authority for interference with the equilibrium force that is wholly and organically inherent and that operates naturally as a divine force.

We are at a threshold in human history. That threshold is the transition from interventionism—which lacks moral authority—to trust in the equilibrium force that exists as a divine institution (for lack of a better term) as part of God's creation of human beings 'in His Image.' We are at the threshold of understanding how to establish a divine civilization in its fullness. We are at a threshold that was not achievable in the past.

Selected Exercises

1. Explain why society is not an entity in and of itself.

2. What two things are required to go against the norms of society?

3. Describe the process of norms becoming laws.

4. Describe social cooperation as the 'ultimate end' accomplished by achieving the consciousness of the oneness of mankind.

5. Discuss law and justice in contrast to ego-driven law and injustice.

6. What is the difference between codified customary law and common law?

7. Describe political anarchy in a positive way.

Chapter 3
A New Perspective

The Model

PREAMBLE

"Hell no!" If life is worth living then life is about living energetically and with passion. Forget all of the nonsense. It simply cannot get in the way—because there is too much at stake. And so, throw aside the dogmas and pooh-pooh the orthodoxy. There is no future in living in the past and there is no future like the here and now: "Go for it!"

INCUBATION

"Each individual is the only and final arbiter in matters concerning his own satisfaction and happiness."[45, p. 13] This quote by Ludwig von Mises summarizes very well the concept of liberty and justice. My job in this chapter is to further elucidate upon this theme in a cohesive way such that the literature of classical liberalism and the work that I have done on the macroeconomics, microeconomics, and ethical economics of the divine economy are all brought together. "No science can avoid abstract concepts, and he who abhors them should stay away from science and see whether and how he can go through life without them."[43, p. 57] And so it is this theoretical exposé, that is about to be unfolded, that will carry us past the critical threshold mentioned at the end of Chapter 2.

We start with the perfectly proportioned concept of a circle to represent economic equilibrium which is also referred to as the divine economy (Diagram 3a).

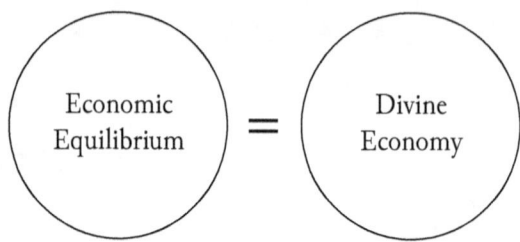

Diagram 3a: Divine Economy Theory Identity

How does this circle come in contact with other elements of human civilization in a two dimensional graphic representation? It is either intersected or it comes in contact at the tangent (Diagram 3b).

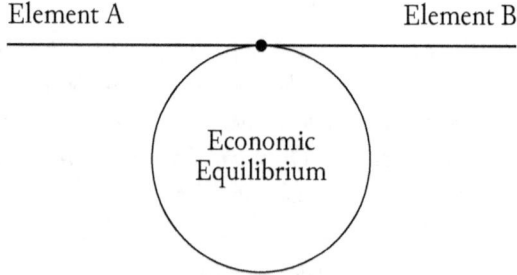

Diagram 3b: Interface of Divine Economy with the Elements of Human Civilization

Tangency represents the single and therefore pure relationship between the circle (equilibrium) and the element.

In a sense there is a balance at that single point. Another way to represent the idea of balance would be to show the elements of human civilization teetering on a fulcrum as shown in Diagram 3c.

This is the starting point for our analysis of the liberty and justice of economic equilibrium (Diagram 3d).

We will return to this progression of steps at the end of this chapter.

The model being developed in this chapter is the fourth in a sequence of four. The first model, laid out in detail in *MORE THAN LAISSEZ-FAIRE*[33], was the macroeconomic model (Diagram 3e):

Implied in the model is my redefinition of praxeology as the study of purposeful action by spiritual beings. Since this redefinition is of

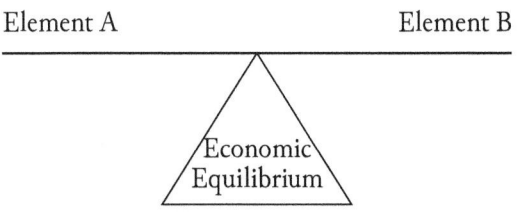

Diagram 3c: The Divine Economy Fulcrum

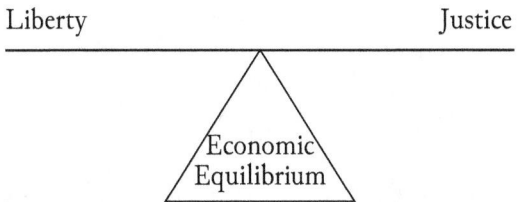

Diagram 3d: The Liberty and Justice of the Divine Economy

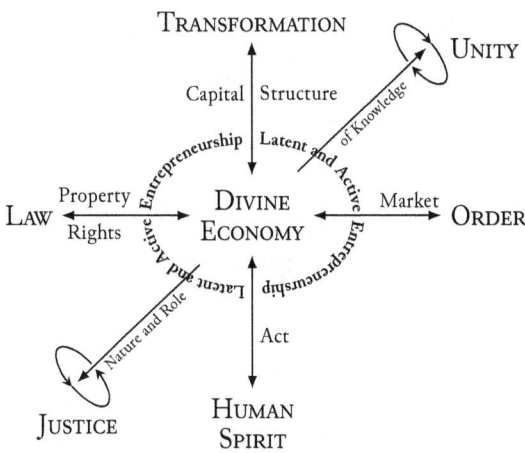

Diagram 3e: The Complete Divine Economy Model

major significance I altered the model to highlight the importance of this redefinition (Diagram 3f).

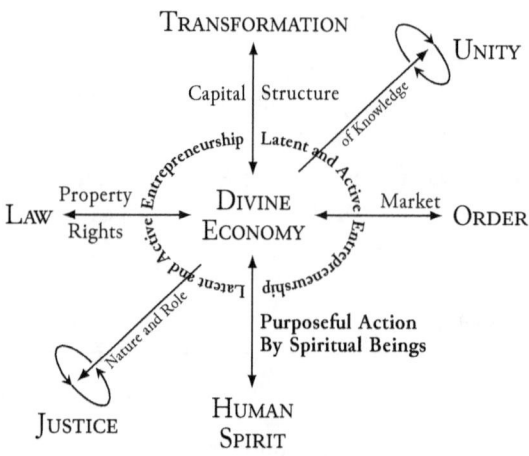

Diagram 3f: The Model with New Definition of Praxeology

The implication, then, is that the act itself is divine (in other words, performed by a spiritual being) which adds great meaning to the simple, central, vertical, Human Spirit/Transformation portion of the model (Diagram 3g). In a sense, it simply and profoundly represents the human reality.

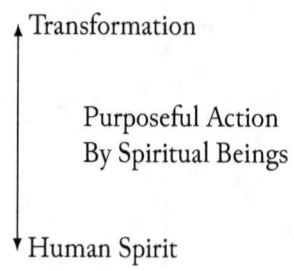

Diagram 3g: We'll Call It the Human Reality

The macro model is dynamic, not static, and so to represent changes over time we have Diagram 3h.

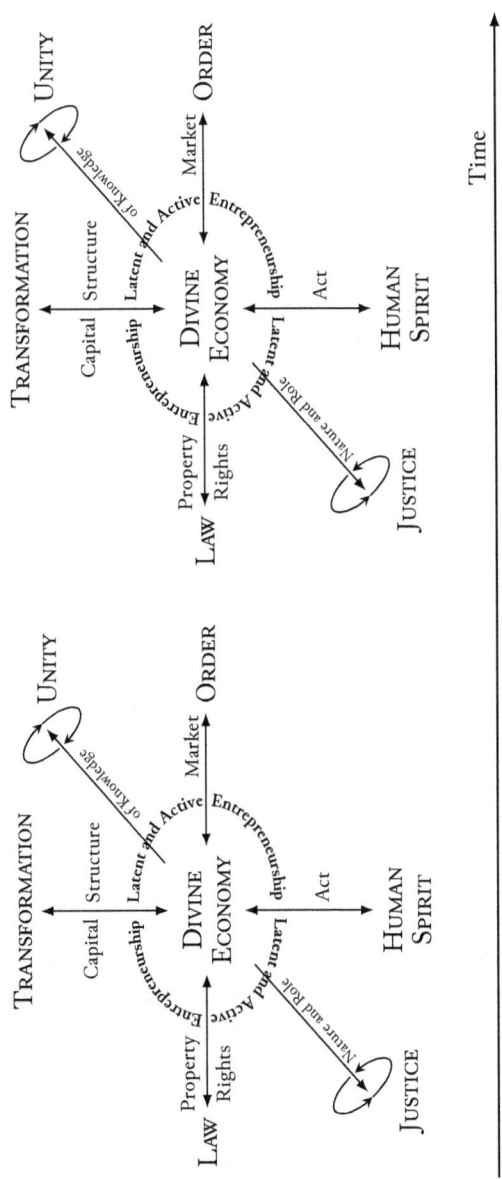

Diagram 3h: The Complete Divine Economy Model Over Time

As a shorthand method of representing this movement we just show the movement of the Nature and Role of Knowledge axis (Diagram 3i), which importantly gives emphasis to the nature and role of knowledge in a human civilization.

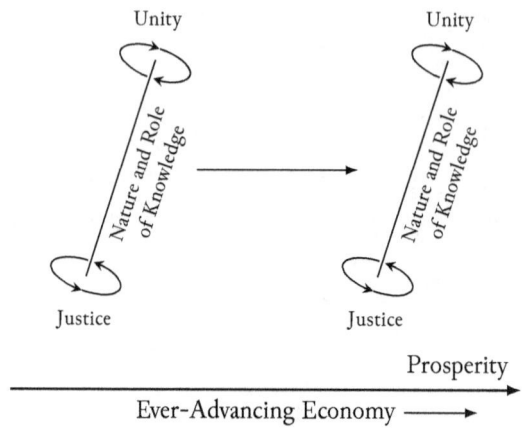

Diagram 3i: Shorthand Version of the Divine Economy Model Over Time

Here is an interesting quote of Ludwig von Mises: "Metaphysics and theology are not, as the positivists pretend, products of an activity unworthy of Homo sapiens, remnants of mankind's primitive age that civilized people ought to discard. They are a manifestation of man's unappeasable craving for knowledge." [41, p. 120] Especially important for us to consider now is this movement of the Justice/Unity axis, which is another name for this axis. It can also be regarded as the axis of the oneness of the world of humanity.

Let's step back. Economics is the science of the study of the means to attain the ends. Along these lines I am now going to suggest that we take a slightly different perspective when looking at the complete model given in Diagram 3e. Further developing the ideas given in Diagram 3f and in Diagram 3g and applying this new definition of praxeology, I found another gem in the model. With all of this in mind, while looking at Diagram 3f imagine that the Human Spirit/Transformation (vertical) axis represents the human reality; in other words, it captures the essence of what we are and what we are doing. The Law/Order (horizontal) axis represents the means, that is, what we have to have for us to get where we are going (law and order, respectively). And finally the Justice/Unity axis represents the ends, what it is that we want (justice and unity, respectively).

As soon as we talk about ends we enter into the realm of ethics but since ethics and economics are inseparable they can both be explored and examined at the same time scientifically. Ends and means are not discretely or absolutely distinct, nor are they independent, so we need to use logic and curiosity to advance our understanding. Means and ends can and do morph into each other to some extent.

TABERNACLE

Continuing along these lines let's consider another perspective. Humans use means to attain ends. In other words Human Spirit/Transformation (human reality) uses Law (means) to bring about Order (ends). And Human Spirit/Transformation (human reality) uses Justice (means) to bring about Unity (ends). The ultimate end which is composed of Order and Unity is social cooperation, which is also a means, as identified by Henry Hazlitt in *The Foundations of Morality* [26, p. 356].

Freeing ourselves up to investigate at the same time both ethics (ends) and economics (means) makes sense since they are intertwined in the real world. Unless unshackled from the restrictions mandated by orthodoxy—noticeably so prior to the emergence of divine economy theory—then many fruits will be left undiscovered.

The Nature and Role of Knowledge axis is quite fascinating. It is a vector that extends to infinity in both directions indicating that there is not and never will be a scarcity of knowledge. Once placed in the model it intersects and interacts with the innumerable means of the real world (Diagram 3j)!

Imagine this axis spinning at phenomenal rates so as to accommodate the transference of information at lightning speed (the internet, for example). "The nature of a scarce resource is that use by one person excludes use by another; but you don't need to own the information that guides your action in order to have successful action. For example, two people can make a cake at the same time. They each have to have their own ingredients, but they can use the same recipe at the same time. Material progress is made over time in human society because

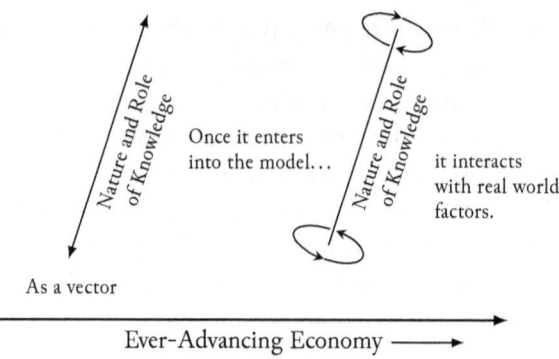

Diagram 3j: The Spinning Knowledge Vector

information is not scarce. It can be infinitely multiplied, learned, taught, and built on. The more patterns, recipes, causal laws that are known add to the stock of knowledge available to all actors and act as a greater and greater wealth multiplier by allowing actors to engage in ever-more efficient and productive actions. It is a good thing that ideas are infinitely reproducible, not a bad thing. There is no need to impose artificial scarcity on these things to make them more like scarce resources, which, unfortunately, are scarce. Knowledge is power because it guides action. It opens up a wider, richer universe of possibilities: it allows human actors to choose from a wider array of ends, and from a wider, richer set of means to achieve one's preferred ends."[32]

In the context of the means/ends conversation what we have is: knowledge + means potentially leads to the attainment of ends. This is the ever-present economic problem! The solution to the problem is inherently a part of the divine economy—purposeful human action. How can I best describe the catalyst of the process—the driving force that is hidden underneath the solution? Entrepreneurship! Entrepreneurs are visionaries that cause the Justice/Unity axis to move to the right (Diagram 3k).

Whoosh! Now we have entered into the divine microeconomy. The entrepreneur is the one who is alert. He or she is alert to the new (mingled with the old) knowledge and is alert to the scarcity of resources. As I described in *The Human Essence of Economics*[34, p. 67]

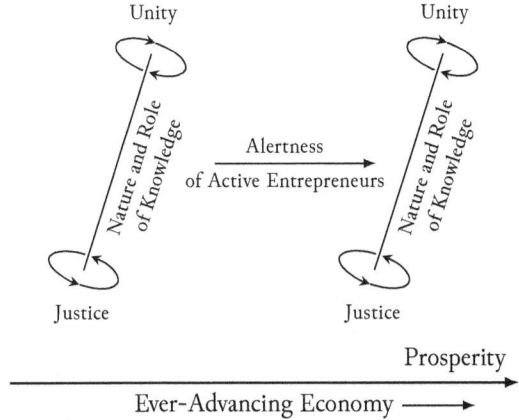

Diagram 3k: Entrepreneurs as the Driving Force

all humans are entrepreneurs, either latent or active, and those that are active have ignited the divine spark as shown in Diagram 3l.

Then I introduced the shorthand version of the divine spark which displayed a radial symmetry and then, next, the divine spark was fully incorporated into (the second model of the sequence of four) the Complete Divine Microeconomy Model (Diagram 3m).

Alertness is another way of saying 'seeking after truth.' It certainly has an intellectual component but it also has a spiritual component which has been unnecessarily neglected by those scientists that are still shackled to some extent by orthodoxy. The seat of all value is the

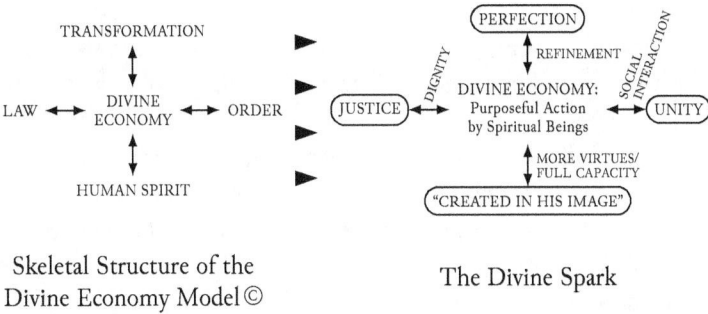

Diagram 3l: The Divine Spark and Its Derivation

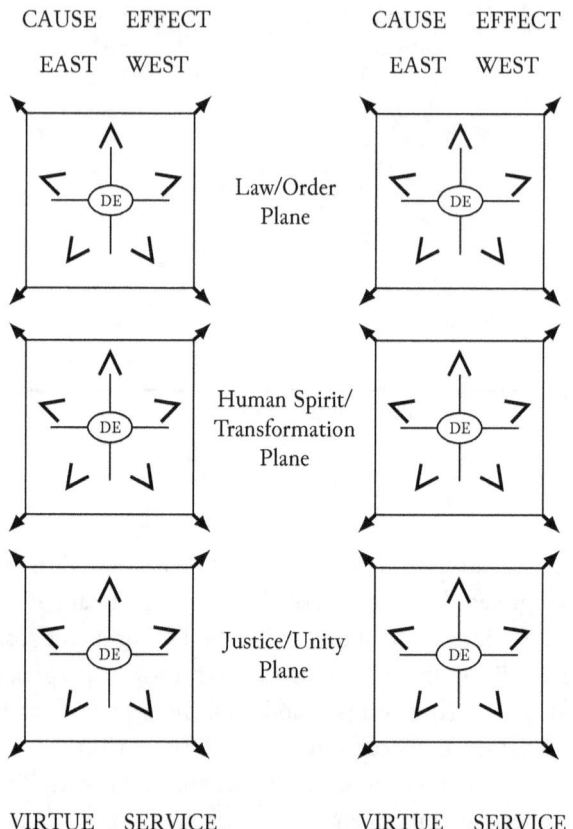

Diagram 3m: The Complete Divine Microeconomy Model

appearance of the virtues or attributes of God in all material things and as the essential component of all human action. It is the appearance of these virtues, and the attraction that they create, that brings about both justice and unity.

First of all, since we are investigating justice let's go ahead and consider justice at the point of the ignition of the divine spark. Alertness of the entrepreneur is the exercising of the most basic human right, the independent investigation of truth. Equally as significant is the fact that it is because of this entrepreneurship (alertness) that transformation takes place, not only at the level of the individual but also within the economy and within the society. To clarify the importance of justice, it is justice that inextricably links the interests of the individual with those of society. It is, therefore, extremely important for the light of justice to reach and to surround the entire arena of entrepreneurship.

Whoosh! This is now the transition from microeconomics into the realm of ethical economics. The infinite nature of the Nature and Role of Knowledge vector is immutably tied to the Covenant of God. It can be said that God's covenant to humankind is that God would always guide and provide for humankind. That flow (of knowledge and bounty) is essentially infinite (and eternal). Yet it is constrained by the world as we know it. It is this world as we know it and our ability to change it over time that is captured in the Complete Model of the Ethics of the Divine Economy[35, p. 44], the third of the series of four models.

To understand the Complete Model of the Ethics of the Divine Economy we first focus our attention on the central, **vertical** axis of the divine economy model (Diagram 3n).

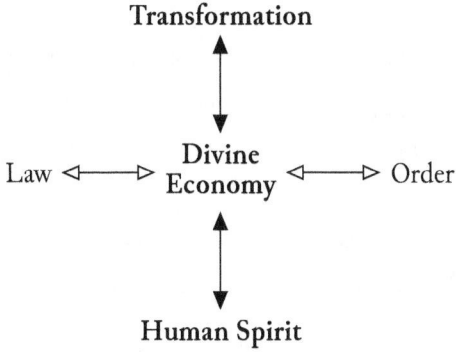

Diagram 3n: The Ethical Strand of the Divine Economy Model

Next, as was developed in detail in *ETHICAL ECONOMICS for Today and Tomorrow...* [35], the model of the ethical economy—confined by its constraints—is shown as it comes in contact with the ethical knowledge delivered as part of the Covenant of God. Diagram 3o shows how the divine economy is the conduit (divine economy ⟷ divine economy) for the influence of the ethical teachings of the Manifestations of God, to bring about changes at the micro and macro level.

The outcome of divine revelation—which inherently contains knowledge about the divine economy—is a divine civilization.

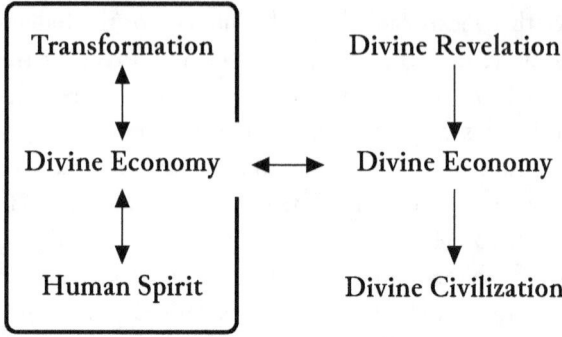

Diagram 3o: Model of the Ethics of the Divine Economy

If not the appearance of a dynamic divine civilization, at least an ever-advancing civilization appears—all depending upon the strength of the Covenant of God in that Day. Diagram 3p shows the Complete Model of the Ethics of the Divine Economy by adding and incorporating the concept of the Covenant of God which is accomplished by incorporating a portion of the symbol of the 'Greatest Name.'

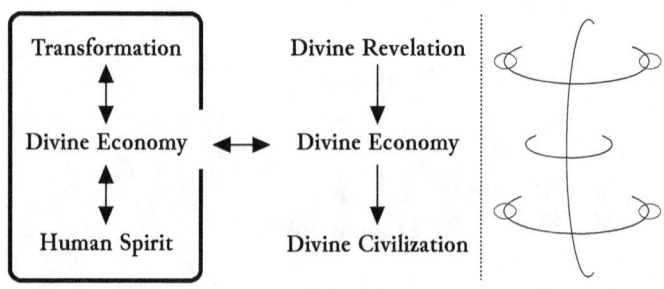

Diagram 3p: Complete Model of the Ethics of the Divine Economy

The primary source of ethics required for an ever-advancing civilization comes from the Manifestations of God and it is the impact of Their Teachings that leads to and spiritualizes social cooperation. Again we see the importance of the Covenant when we consider its ability or inability to withstand the assault of the ego-driven. If it is strong and inviolable we get a divine civilization, whereas if it is violated the best we can hope for is an ever-advancing civilization that is constantly being whittled away under the attack of the ego-driven.

ASSAY

As we move through the sequence of models I think it can be said that we are now feeling a sense of appreciation for and a mounting desire for justice. The divine spark has ignited our alertness to discover and discern justice. It is my job in this chapter and at this point to bring to the forefront the justice aspect of the divine economy model.

If we go back to the skeletal structure of the divine economy model and this time place our focus and emphasis on the central, **horizontal**, Law/Order axis we can begin the process (Diagram 3q).

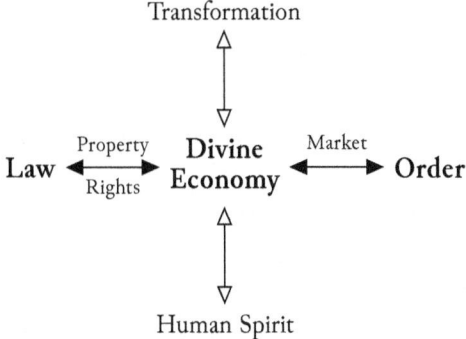

Diagram 3q: The Justice Aspect of the Divine Economy Model

"The connection between economics and the law is implied, but it is rarely regarded by economists as a special object worthy of their research."[37, p. 50] Keeping in mind the concept of reciprocity, the immediate implication is that laws bring about order. The source of the laws determines the type of order. Rotten law/order brings about rotten order/law, whereas good law brings about a good order, and whereas divine law brings about divine order (Diagram 3r).

Already clearly identified in the divine economy model is the starting point for laws—property rights. The essence of property rights is this identity: property rights are human rights and human rights are property rights. In other words, the human reality is the most precious of all considerations.

The principal provider of order and of social cooperation—operating and expressed through the language of exchange activities—that fills

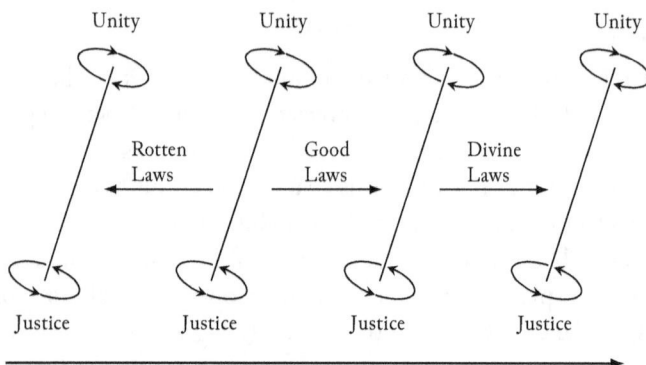

Diagram 3r: Ego-Driven Versus Divine Laws

the lives of everyone everywhere as part of the market process, is the 'market' itself.

Justice implies protective respect for both the human reality and for the healthy freedom of expression of the human reality. To get a better grasp of all of these things—honoring the human reality and its expression—we need to acknowledge the inseparability of liberty and justice. Balancing liberty and justice is the essential key.

And so, necessarily, there is a very meaningful relationship between law and the inseparability of liberty and justice. Developed law, over time, resulting from search and discovery (only if it has been uninfluenced by the ego-driven) is compatible with both liberty and justice. Probably you or I do not believe that is what we have. But let's assume that is what has occurred and then have fun with that assumption. Liberty and justice create order and having order leads to the refinement of liberty and justice. This cycle is circular just like the letter O in the word 'Order' and according to the divine economy theory the circle is the symbol of economic equilibrium (Diagram 3s).

Although this ideal equilibrium process just described is valid, the starting point is not. In fact, laws have been influenced by the ego-driven and the whole structure of society is the rotten fruit of those laws. The laws need erased, and understandably, the structures built upon those laws are of no value.

Of course replacing the laws and its structures with nothing or

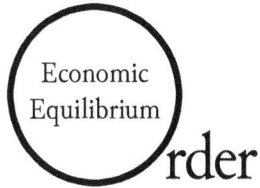

Diagram 3s: The Order of Economic Equilibrium

just replacing the laws and its structures with a different set of ego-driven laws and structures makes no sense. Only if the Covenant of God provides us with a divine alternative can we be better off than we are now. It is this rational insight that is the foundation of a true human society.

In the Complete Model of the Ethics of the Divine Economy (Diagram 3p) we saw the incorporation of the Covenant of God. At that point only a portion of the 'Greatest Name' was used. What happens if we add the divine microeconomy concept of the divine spark? Remember the radial symmetry of the divine spark? It represents the radial symmetry of the human temple (the head, two arms, and two legs [Diagram 3t]).

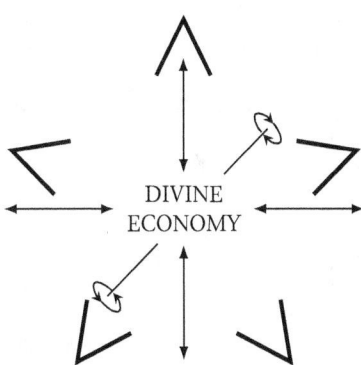

Diagram 3t: The Symmetry of the Divine Spark

Symbolically, it is the divine spark that ignites the human spirit.

Before completing the Model of the Justice of the Divine Economy I want to show you the rest of the 'Greatest Name', and describe how it fits into the model (Diagram 3u).

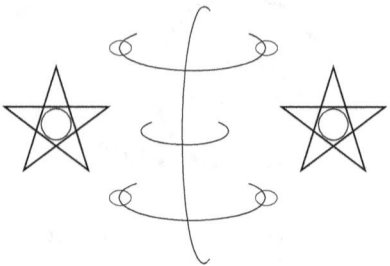

Diagram 3u: The Greatest Name

Notice the two stars. Initially think of them as fulfilling the central, horizontal, Law/Order axis of the divine economy model; the left one representing Law and the right one representing Order. But actually these stars historically represent the Twin Manifestations of God in this Day and so they do indeed connect us very specifically to the Covenant of God. Now we can return to continue with the Law/Order analogy. The Laws that They brought will bring the Order of a divine civilization because the Covenant is strong and inviolable, unlike in the past.

With all of this in mind I now present to you the Model of the Justice of the Divine Economy, the fourth of the series of four models.

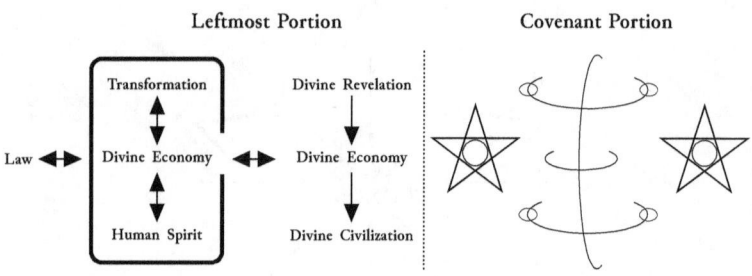

Diagram 3v: The Complete Model of the Justice of the Divine Economy

In contrast to the Complete Model of the Ethics of the Divine Economy (Diagram 3p) notice that Law appears in the leftmost portion of the model and as the leftmost star in the 'Greatest Name' (Covenant) portion. Also because Law and Order are both a part of the rightmost Covenant portion of the model (the left and right stars, respectively) take notice that the other appearance of Order is in the leftmost portion as part of the divine civilization process (DR → DE ↔ DC). It turns out that justice is the key ingredient opening a pathway of reciprocity between the divine economy and the divine civilization and vice versa.

The 'Greatest Name' emblem by itself can easily be imagined as a seal to be pressed into wax to seal the deal. This conceptualization fits well with the concept of a covenant (agreement) and it also fits well with the concept of a contractual society. In other words, the economy operates properly when it is contractual.

To close this chapter we bring back the sequence of Diagrams 3a to 3d but complete it using all of the knowledge thus far contained in this chapter.

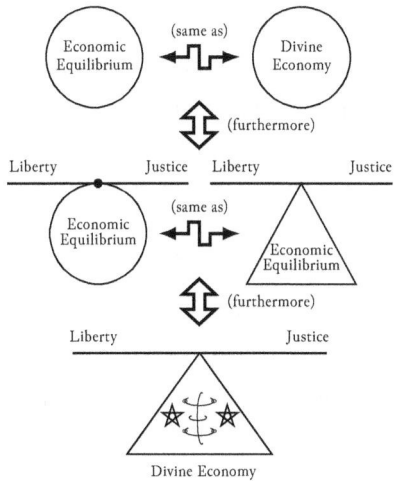

Diagram 3w: The Liberty and Justice of the Divine Economy Sequence

Diagram 3w shows the progression of thought from the initial concept of the divine economy as a synonym for economic equilibrium to its coming in contact with the human civilization elements of liberty and justice. It becomes clear that liberty and justice are maintained in relative balance by the forces of economic equilibrium, and are contemporarily forced to work against the ego-driven forces. The perfect balance of liberty and justice in the divine economy is the result of the removal of ego-driven intervention, replaced providentially with the divine laws and order provided by the strong and inviolable Covenant given to us in this Day.

With regards the divine economy theory I refer you to a quote from Ludwig von Mises, "What matters is not whether a doctrine is new, but whether it is sound."[42, p. 53] Imagine the benefits to the economy and to human civilization that will ultimately result from a healthy injection of both certitude and certainty!

Selected Exercises

1. Give another example where a circle is used as a significant symbol.

2. Describe the conceptual progression that occurs from Diagram 3e through Diagram 3g.

3. Give an example of a "fruit" that will be "left undiscovered" if the inseparability and intertwining of economics and ethics is not understood.

4. Use Diagram 3j to discuss intellectual property.

5. Describe how "entrepreneurship" is a window that permits the bridging of economic science and spirituality.

6. How relieved are you to now have a clear connection between economics and law?

7. Describe the importance of recognizing the human reality with its connection to property rights, and the market as the principal provider of order and social cooperation.

8. Use Diagram 3v to describe, as thoroughly as you can, law and order.

9. Comment on the quote of Ludwig von Mises [ref. 42, p. 53] with regards the divine economy theory.

Chapter 4
Classical Liberalism

The Groundwork of Liberty and Justice

Preamble

With powers of the intellect growing stronger every day and with a prowess to imbibe the knowledge that is coming from all directions in the rapidly evolving civilization, it is time to gain mastery over the sphere of knowledge. Today access to knowledge is almost instantaneous and universal and so the process is one of sifting, using a critical eye and a keen mind. To accomplish this task the essential ingredient is perception: "What knowledge is useful knowledge?"

Incubation

We find ourselves at an elevated theoretical position where not only are ethics and economics inseparable but also law and justice are tightly woven into the economic fabric of life. Just like when examining the natural world, the deeper we go into the inner workings the more we need to understand the big picture. Probing deeply into liberty and justice opens a broad vista of human civilization over its entire time horizon. Cause and effect is still the theoretical basis of our understanding but our ability to apply science at a very high level—pushing the envelop—is being tested by this theoretical position.

A perfect example is the earth itself and all of its differentiated resources and climates. Add to this mix the rich and nearly infinite diversity of human personalities. And yet the direction that all this is going is towards unity! Sure, it is a relatively slow process, but then again, look how fast it is occurring relative to geological change.

Certainly unity could just appear without the painstaking process if it were pre-ordained to be so but there would be no semblance of human reality in that shallow figment of imagination. Not much different are the vain imaginings of those who are ego-driven, whose intervention disregards the way the human reality expresses itself voluntarily in the world. Sure, there may be 'unity' under totalitarianism but it is oppressive and soulless.

It is not a mere coincidence that the earth's resources are differential or that humans are diverse. It is no mere coincidence that humans have an affinity for social cooperation. Unity is a reality but it only has meaning because it is understood and it is only understood because it can be and is learned. Yet the best means to learn what it is that we are supposed to learn is through the liberty and justice emanations originating from the divine equilibrium force.

Divine economy theory is broad enough to permit us to consider all of these things. To begin we can never lose sight of the ever-present and omnipotent equilibrium force. Impatience and/or arrogance must be purged from our minds. In other words, all of the cherished human identities and principles and aspirations have an inherent balance. They are in harmony. There is symmetry among them and also reciprocity. It is equilibrium that allows their full expression and power and it is equilibrium that is the natural force that is both hidden and manifest.

All of existence has meaning because existence is recognized by human beings. How incredibly significant human life is, therefore! This is the first principle of the "Ten Principles of Classical Liberalism" as stated by G. Stolyarov II: "The life of each individual is an absolute and universal moral value. No non-aggressive individual's life, liberty, or property may be legitimately sacrificed for any goal."[56] To this add the powerful insight of Ludwig von Mises, "Eternal law regulates everything. In this sense determinism is the epistemological basis of the human search for knowledge. Man cannot even conceive the image of an undetermined universe. In such a world there could not be any awareness of material things and their changes. It would appear a senseless chaos. Nothing could be identified and distinguished from anything else. Nothing could be expected and predicted. In the midst of such an environment man would be as helpless as if spoken to in an unknown language. No action could be designed, still less put into execution. Man is what he is because he lives in a world of regularity and has the mental power to conceive the relation of cause and effect."[45, p. 74]

Because each human being is an entity that dwells on Earth part of his or her identity consists of property ownership. The second principle is that "Every individual owns his body, his mind, and the labor thereof, including the physical objects legitimately obtained through such labor." The other part of this identity is that property rights are human rights and human rights are property rights. To this add these words of wisdom, "The continued existence of society depends upon private property, and since men have need of society, they must hold fast to the institution of private property to avoid injuring their own interests as well as the interests of everyone else. For society can continue to exist only on the foundation of private property. Whoever champions the latter champions by the same token the preservation of the social bond that unites mankind, the preservation of culture and civilization. He is an apologist and defender of society, culture, and civilization, and because he desires them as ends, he must also desire and defend the one means that leads to them, namely, private property."[46, p. 87]

Notice the progression from the identity of an individual to the rights of the individual and their interconnectedness. Implied is the establishing and granting of rights and these can be best described as God-given rights. Principle Three (I interchanged Principle Three and Principle Four) is as follows: "The rights of an individual to life, liberty, and property are inherent to that individual's nature. They are not *granted* by other human beings, and they cannot be taken away by any entity."

It was necessary to spell out the details in these first three principles but they can easily be regarded as a single foundational definition of an independent, unique, and fully-endowed individual. Principle One (L for life) and Principle Two (PR = HR for property rights=human rights) and Principle Three (GGR for God-given rights) can be given a shorthand symbol of L : PR = HR : GGR, essentially representing a fully-endowed individual.

In search for happiness he or she embarks on life's endeavors and the essence of this is captured in Principle Four: "Every individual has the right to pursue activities for the betterment of his life—including its material, intellectual, and emotional aspects—by using his own body and property, as well as the property of consenting others." This pursuance of means to attain ends is optimized when there is economic liberty (given the symbol **EL**). In other words, we exercise purposeful action in the surrounding world that has been created for our use, in cooperation with others.

TABERNACLE

It is at this point where the companion of liberty takes its place as a great counterbalance. Equilibrium forces tend to bring about a balance between liberty and justice. And so the natural restraint to unbounded liberty, that protects life (**L**), property rights (**PR** = **HR**), God-given rights (**GGR**) and economic liberty is non-aggressive self defense as stated in Principle Five: "The initiation of physical force, the threat of such force, or fraud against any individual is never permissible—irrespective of the position and character of the initiator. However, proportionate force may be used to retaliate and defend against aggression."

There is a naturalness to the protective shelter of justice which can either be enhanced by or undermined and corrupted by government. For enhancement it is essential that life (**L**), property rights (**PR** = **HR**), God-given rights (**GGR**), economic liberty (**EL**), and non-aggressive self-defense (**SD**) become incorporated into the structure of a limited government and strictly adhered to. These principles serve as a litmus test to be continually used to detect corruption of the government and by the government. Limited government (**LG**) is the only way there can be justice if government is made a part of society. This is Principle Six: "The sole fundamental purpose of government is to protect the rights of individuals by engaging in actions specifically delegated to the government by its constituents. Government is not the same as society, nor is the government entitled to sacrifice some non-aggressive individuals to advance the well-being of others." Commenting on government and liberty Mises proclaims: "Government is a guarantor of liberty and is compatible with liberty only if its range is adequately restricted to the preservation of what is called economic freedom."[48, p. 283]

No matter how universally accepted the pattern of society there will always be those who are alert to injustices and there will always be those whose beliefs are not perfectly compatible with the social pattern. A significant test of liberty and justice—permitting the force of equilibrium to be the ultimate arbiter of reciprocity and harmony—is the respect given within a society to the rights of the freedom of speech and the freedom of religious belief (**FSFF**). Is the water clean and pure or is it tainted? Apply the test of Principle Seven: "Every individual has the absolute right to think and express any ideas. Thought and speech are never equivalent to force or violence and ought never to be restricted or to be subject to coercive penalties. Specifically, coercion and censorship on the basis of religious or political ideas are not acceptable under any circumstances." This is the attitude of peaceful prosperity: "Liberalism limits its concern entirely and exclusively to earthly life and earthly endeavor. The kingdom of religion, on the other hand, is not of this world. Thus, liberalism and religion could both exist side by side without their spheres' touching.... Liberalism proclaims tolerance for every religious faith and every metaphysical belief, not out of indifference for these 'higher' things, but from the conviction that the assurance of peace within society must take precedence over everything and everyone."[46, pp. 55–56]

We have built up a series of principles that can be symbolized and juxtaposed next to each other to heighten our understanding. For example we modeled a fully-endowed individual as **L : PR = HR : GGR**. We said that the individual (**L : PR = HR : GGR**) freely and faithfully (**FSFF**) pursues his or her endeavors naturally as **EL** (economic liberty). At this point in our exposition we benefit from diagrammatic representations. As soon as we consider economic liberty we also must bring a degree of justice into the picture as shown in Diagram 4a by adding **SD** (self-defense).

$$\frac{EL}{L : PR = HR : GGR/FSFF + SD}$$

Diagram 4a: Economic Liberty with a Degree of Justice

A fully-endowed individual that functions freely and voluntarily in society can be represented by Diagram 4b.

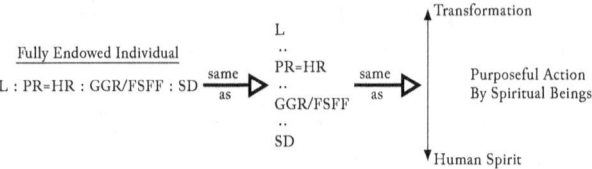

Diagram 4b: The Human Reality Potential within Economic Liberty

In Diagram 4c limited government (**LG**) is added which makes the distinction of the balancing of liberty and justice more obvious to see in the diagram, mirroring the real world need for clarity in a limited government society, and as societies evolve. Notice that societal liberty is associated with economic liberty (**EL**) which is both ethical (**L : PR = HR : GGR**) and just (**+SD**).

LIBERTY	JUSTICE
EL	LG
L : PR=HR : GGR/FSFF + SD	

Diagram 4c: Liberty and Justice Is a Protection from Goverment

The next principle, Principle Eight, pertains to the free market and it is pivotal since the free market is the very essence and embodiment of both liberty and justice in an ethical society. Stated: "Commerce, technology, and science are desirable, liberating forces that are capable of alleviating historic ills, improving the quality of human life, and morally elevating human beings. The complete freedom of trade, innovation, and thought should be preserved and supported for all human beings in the world." With this in mind, "The market steers the capitalistic economy. It directs each individual's activities into those channels in which he best serves the wants of his fellow-men. The market alone puts the whole social system of private ownership of the means of production and free enterprise in order and provides it with sense and meaning."[42, p. 72]

Diagram 4d emphasizes the justice aspect of the free market (**FM**). Depending on the needs of a particular society the free market is wholly sufficient to provide complete justice; but some societies may include limited government as part of the means to attain justice. All of these elements of human civilization are brought into harmony, reciprocity, and symmetry by the omnipresent, omnipotent, and omniscient equilibrating force.

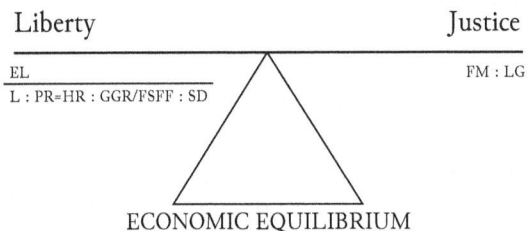

Diagram 4d: Liberty and Justice of Economic Equilibrium

Here is another internal observation about these eight principles. There is a very strong reciprocity between **L** (Principle One – Life) and **SD** (Principle Five – self-defense). Notice the symmetry and reciprocity between **GGR** (Principle Three – God-given rights) and **FSFF** (Principle Seven – freedom of speech and faith). Likewise there is a necessary reciprocity between **PR = HR** (Principle Two – property rights) and **LG** (Principle Six – limited government). And very powerful indeed is the harmony, reciprocity and symmetry between **EL** (Principle Four – economic liberty) and **FM** (Principle Eight – free market).

Assay

"By their fruits ye shall know them"[39] applies to individuals and can also be used to evaluate societies. What are the fruits of a civilization that tries to balance liberty and justice? What are the fruits of a society that applies these first eight principles?

We are not quite finished since there are ten principles, but these last two emphasize the fruits of the philosophy of classical liberalism just like the first three embodied the essence of a fully-endowed individual.

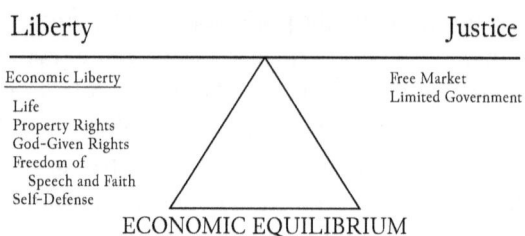

Diagram 4e: Description of the First Eight Principles of Classical Liberalism

Since human life and human expression and human rights are to be respected and appreciated in classical liberalism it is the unhampered flow of God's grace that is allowed to operate. No ego-driven human intervention, distorting the force of equilibrium, is permitted. Freed from the shackles of prejudices and manmade restrictions everyone enjoys the fruits of Principle Nine: "Accidents of birth, geography, or ancestry do not define an individual and should not result in manmade restrictions of that individual's rights or opportunities. Every individual should be judged purely on his or her personal qualities, including accomplishments, character, and knowledge." Liberty and justice unites all human beings.

The culmination of this highly evolved civilization that perfectly balances liberty and justice is at the same time a gift to and a responsibility of all those who are a part of it. Theirs and ours is the privilege and duty to carry forward an ever-advancing civilization. Such a wonderful challenge is at our fingertips, nay rather, it turns out that it is closer than our life vein!

Unknown to us is the true potential of this unfathomably great being (our own selves), created 'in His Image'. "A technological invention is not something material. It is the product of a mental process, of reasoning and conceiving new ideas. The tools and machines may be called material, but the operation of the mind which created them is certainly spiritual."[45, p. 109] The problems that we face are ephemeral just like the problems of the past and the problems of the future were and will be ephemeral. "That which was applicable to human needs during the early history of the race can neither meet nor satisfy the demands of this day, this period of newness and consummation. Humanity has emerged from its former state of limitation and preliminary training. Man must now become imbued with new virtues and powers, new moral standards, new capacities."[1, p. 9] Notably and nobly, men and women are the supremely talismanic creatures. Only when burdened by the artificial, narrow-minded, and short-sighted vain imaginings of the ego-driven will our unending progress be impeded. Successfully counteracting ego-driven interpretation and intervention will yield the superbly luscious fruits of a classical liberalism society which can be discerned from reading Principle Ten: "There are no 'natural' or desirable limits to human potential for good, and there is no substantive problem that is necessarily unsolvable by present or future human knowledge, effort, and technology. It is a moral imperative for humans to expand their mastery of the universe indefinitely and in such a manner as will reinforce the survival and flourishing of all non-aggressive individuals."

"When social cooperation is intensified by enlarging the field in which there is division of labor or when legal protection and the safeguarding of peace are strengthened, the incentive is the desire of all those concerned to improve their own conditions. In striving after his own—rightly understood—interests the individual works toward an intensification of social cooperation and peaceful intercourse."[26, p. 312]

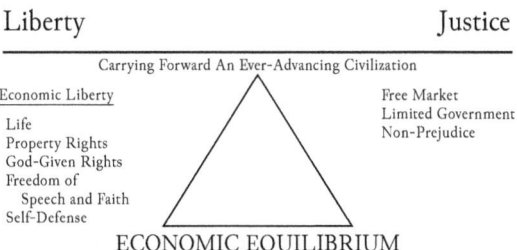

Liberty   Justice

Carrying Forward An Ever-Advancing Civilization

Economic Liberty   Free Market
Life   Limited Government
Property Rights   Non-Prejudice
God-Given Rights
Freedom of
    Speech and Faith
Self-Defense
                    ECONOMIC EQUILIBRIUM

Diagram 4f: Complete Description of the Ten Principles of Classical Liberalism

"If these things can be accomplished and if the philosophy of economic liberalism can take hold across the world and further intensify in the areas in which it already has taken hold, then for the first time in human history a truly global economic system will be achieved, bringing unprecedented prosperity and economic progress everywhere."[53]

As you can see, stripping away all of the burdensome laws and regulations that plague our society does not leave a void. There exists an enduring subtle underlying culture of classical liberalism; so there is no need to fear the removal of interventionism. The perfect balance and unerring and all-powerful force of equilibrium is guaranteed. It is when ego-driven interventionism is removed that we will find that we are but one step away from a divine civilization.

Selected Exercises

1. Is L : PR = HR : GGR : SD a good model of a fully-endowed individual?

2. Which principles serve as a litmus test to detect government corruption? Give an example.

3. Is the free market wholly sufficient to bring about justice? Explain.

4. What is the relationship between Principle One and Principle Five; between Principle Two and Principle Six; between Principle Three and Principle Seven; and between Principle Four and Principle Eight? Give at least one specific example of this relationship.

5. According to divine economy theory, what is hampered by ego-driven human intervention?

6. If interventionism is removed what will be left?

Chapter 5
Harmony In 3D: The Covenant

The Model and Liberty & Justice of
the Divine Economy

PREAMBLE

Call it intuition or call it an "inner voice" but do not leave out of the equation the vision-enhancing powers of the spiritual eye. What else can lead to the discovery of the illumination referred to as the "truth?" When that light dawns on the intellect or on the spirit all efforts are rewarded with the much sought-after prize. That prize is discovery. It fires the desire for more knowledge and more discoveries, inspiring: "I want to know the essential verities of life!"

INCUBATION

How strange the world is! How bewildering is our ability to perceive or not to perceive. To some extent it is like standing at the edge of a precipice reaching out with uncertainty towards a branch that would give us access to a whole new realm. Why should we cross when there is still much that is unknown and unexplored on this side? But crossing back and forth offers so much more. "The actual world is a world of permanent change."[44, p. 28]

The natural order and the divine order surround us, intrigue us, nourish us and dwarf us. Yet we are like the catalyst. "There is within the infinite expanse of what is called the universe or nature a small field in which man's conscious conduct can influence the course of events."[41, p. 11]

We already know that conscientiously we all choose liberty and justice and that we can find them to be in balance the closer the natural order mirrors the divine order. From one perspective justice (J) can be seen (Diagram 5a) as the tip of the fulcrum against which all things are weighed.

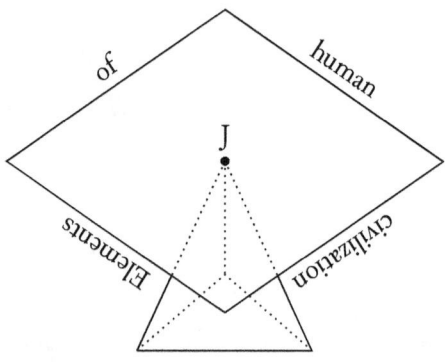

Diagram 5a: Justice and the Elements of Human Civilization

Justice ultimately serves to protect the human reality. Protected, the human spirit acts purposefully and undergoes transformation. Anything that interferes with this process is unjust. Consider another perspective as shown in Diagram 5b.

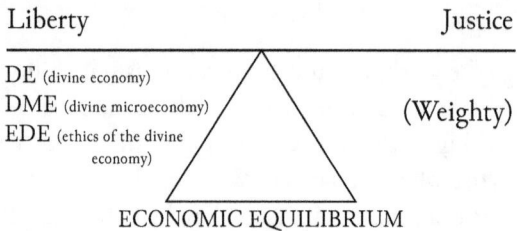

Diagram 5b: The Weightiness of Justice

Notice that there are three symbols on the left which must be offset on the right to keep things in balance. Justice must be 'weighty' to permit the divine economy (DE), the divine microeconomy (DME), and the ethics of the divine economy (EDE) to operate in human civilization. In other words, justice must reign supreme in the period of human history when the human reality is fully protected.

Reciprocity and symmetry are words that contain within them the concept of justice. Just like words function as symbols, so too do diagrams. Consider Diagram 5c.

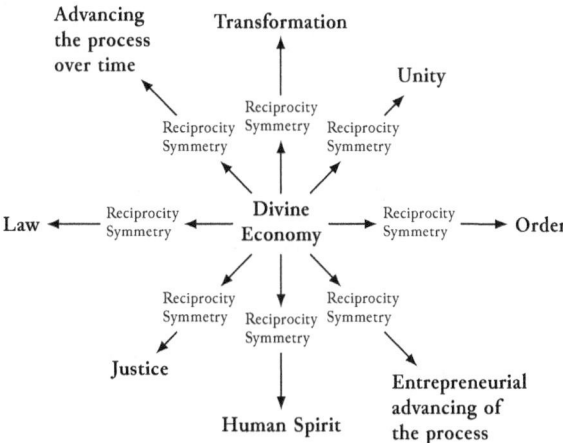

Diagram 5c: Reciprocity and Symmetry Permeate the Divine Economy

The process that is being advanced is the carrying forward of an ever-advancing civilization and as you can see the justice of reciprocity and symmetry is essential and necessary throughout.

Out of the complexity of reality I will pick out one infinitely complex piece: The material world is an objectification of the spiritual world. For instance, we can depend on the appearance each and every year of the springtime, which renews our surroundings because of the impact of the radiant energy of the Sun, and thus each time we enter a new cycle. Also, the entrepreneur discovers that his or her clients prefer clearly written contracts because they are binding and they eliminate or at least minimize uncertainty. The Covenant of God is the spiritual counterpart of both of these objective realities.

With that thought cradled in our mind; for each epoch of human history there is a springtime caused by a renewal generated from the appearance of a Manifestation of God. The appearance is part of the

Covenant of God and in its nature it is contractual. I venture to say that humans deeply value contracts because it emulates this most basic and inherent relationship with their Creator. It turns out that the Covenant binds all things together. In fact, "the axis of the oneness of the world of humanity is the power of the Covenant and nothing else"[2, p. 425] as can be seen in Diagram 5d. The knowledge of unity and the knowledge of justice and the role that unity and justice play in civilization is made much more powerful by the strength and inviolability of the Covenant.

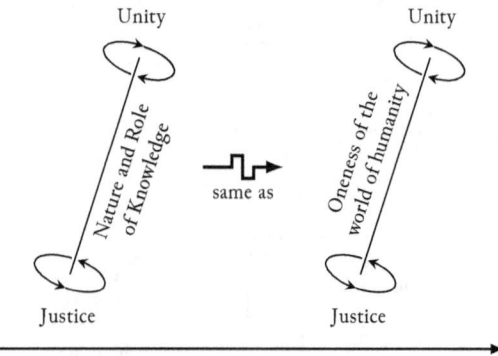

Diagram 5d: The Justice/Unity Axis of the Oneness of the World of Humanity

Diagram 5e is a modification of the Covenant portion of the Model of the Ethics of the Divine Economy (Diagram 3p), achieved by combining it with the information presented in the "Change Over Time" diagram and the "Cyclical Nature of the Model of the Ethics of the Divine Economy" diagram from *Ethical Economics for Today and Tomorrow...* [35, p. 46] The inviolable Covenant symbolized by the Greatest Name is the difference in the DR/DE/DC cycle this time around.

One odd importance of this diagram is that it can be used to explain the formation of communism and the State and nationalism! The epoch of human civilization that received the Dispensation of Jesus the Christ had within it the inherent characteristics of city-states. ʿAbduʾl-Bahá is quoted as saying: "Christ renewed and again revealed the commands of the one God and precepts of human action."[5, p. 154] Had the Covenant of that Dispensation been inviolable a divine civilization with a city-state nature would have developed and history would have been

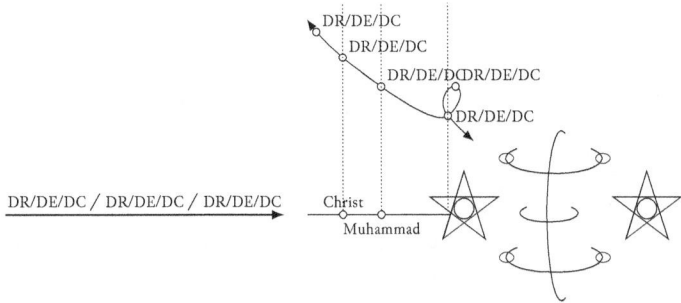

Diagram 5e: A Deeper Examination of the Covenant Portion of the Model

different. Yet since human action was sanctified within the precepts of Christianity the city-state was able to manifest itself in certain ways that resembled the divine civilization when it spread into Western Europe and left a positive and lasting imprint.

One of the deviations during this particular epoch: The origin of communism stems from heretical Christianity.[55, p. 159] Several early clerics succumbed to their own ego-driven interpretations which led them to conclude that property within the city-states should be common and these clerics embarked on social experiments of communism. It was from these origins that sprung other ego-driven interpreters, trying to replicate these heretical experiments. Later on other ego-driven interpreters came along and to them the need for a religious foundation dropped out, yet their avid pursuance of the perverse ideals of communism continued.

The epoch of human civilization that received the Dispensation of Muḥammad cradled within itself the inherent characteristics of nation-hood. Not only that, but the Covenant of the Muhammadan Dispensation was considerably stronger—Muḥammad verbally appointed ʿAlí as His Successor. Just because the Covenant was stronger does not mean that it was inviolable. The stronger the Covenant the greater the tests and the more serious the consequences if the Covenant is violated.

Once the Covenant was violated the means to carry out the true nature of the nation disappeared precisely during this epoch of fundamental nation-building. Instead of having a divine civilization characteristic of the time of nation-building what emerged was an ego-driven alternative. The energies released for the betterment of human civilization produced some marvelous fruits but the inherent potentialities of nation-building were used instead to gain power and led to the formation of the State. Thus we entered into a period of history where, instead of a divine civilization, the alternative attainment was the darkness of nationalism.

But nobody can halt the reappearance of spring! In 1844 it happened again. The First of the Twin Manifestations appeared. And so now we will focus our attention on the emblem of the 'Greatest Name' (Diagram 5f). The star on the left is the Báb. The Báb fulfilled Islam and Heralded the coming of Bahá'u'lláh.

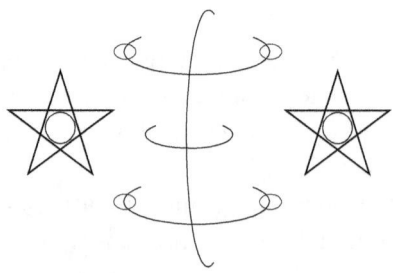

Diagram 5f: The Greatest Name

Regarding how far human civilization had evolved, during the Dispensation of Christ it evolved up to the stage of the city-state. The next leap that was to happen—which was the potential of the divine civilization for that next epoch—was nation-building, but it did not come about properly. However when Islam was fulfilled by the Báb He brought not only the potency that was lost but also the rest of what was needed for the next epoch of human civilization—world order.

The star on the right represents Bahá'u'lláh. He is the Promised One for this Age and it is His inviolable Covenant that will enable humanity to succeed in forming the divine civilization this time around. In other words, the Covenant of Bahá'u'lláh has gotten rid of all ego-driven interpretation of the religion of God!

Science does have a role to play. "The flowering of human society depends on two factors: the intellectual power of outstanding men to conceive sound social and economic theories, and the ability of these or other men to make these ideologies palatable to the majority."[48, p. 864] Mises again wisely puts things into perspective: "Science does not give us absolute and final certainty. It only gives us assurance within the limits of our mental abilities and the prevailing state of scientific thought. A scientific system is but one station in an endlessly progressing search for knowledge. It is necessarily affected by the insufficiency inherent in every human effort. But to acknowledge these facts does not mean that present-day economics is backward. It merely means that economics is a living thing—and to live implies both imperfection and change."[48, p. 7] Divine economy theory is part of this necessary scientific process.

Divine economy theory is a product of the combination of economic science built upon the tradition of classical liberalism and the inspiration of the Covenant of Bahá'u'lláh. "As the Bahá'í community continues to grow it will acquire experts in numerous fields—both by Bahá'ís becoming experts and by experts becoming Bahá'ís. As these experts bring their knowledge and skill to the service of the community and, even more, as they transform their various disciplines by bringing to bear upon them the light of the Divine Teachings, problem after problem now disrupting society will be answered."[57, p. 369] What you find in the divine economy theory is the recognition of the errors in economic science and political science caused by ego-driven interpretation and ego-driven intervention. These errors are completely unnecessary and are completely avoidable. Besides, there is no moral authority for either ego-driven interpretation or ego-driven intervention.

TABERNACLE

Of course I almost always agree with Ludwig von Mises ("economics is a living thing") and now I am going to continue to explore the organic 'living' nature of the economy. Diagram 5g shows a close-up view-from-above of the economic equilibrium force. It starts with justice as the fulcrum as depicted in Diagram 5a. Similar to Diagram 5b the base has three components: the divine economy (DE), the divine microeconomy (DME), and the ethics of the divine economy (EDE). Justice of the divine economy (JDE) is the bearer of the weight.

This implantation of the 'Greatest Name' is very similar to the technique that I used on page 59 in *The HUMAN ESSENCE of Economics*[34] when I implanted the divine spark into the Complete Model of the Divine Microeconomy.

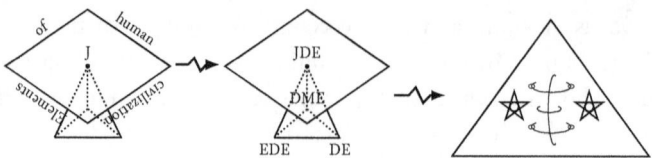

Diagram 5g: Implantation of the Greatest Name

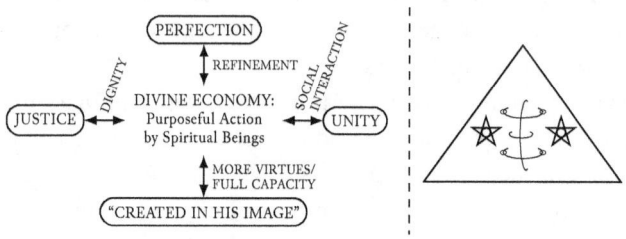

Diagram 5h: Different Divine Economy Perspectives

Let's look at these side by side (Diagram 5h).

Remember that another way to refer to the force of economic equilibrium is to say 'divine economy.' It is clear from Diagram 5g that the triangle with the emblem of the 'Greatest Name' inside is the base of the equilibrium fulcrum. And so you could combine it with the divine spark (Diagram 5i). This is one of the fascinating observations at the microlevel.

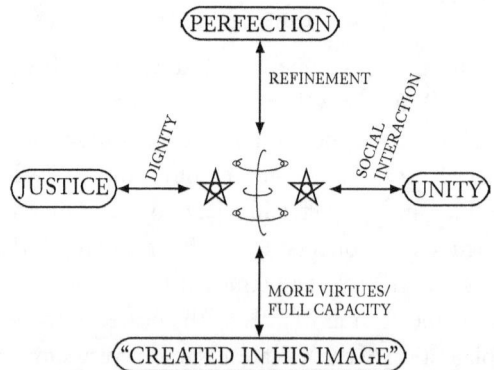

Diagram 5i: Another Divine Spark Perspective

To further this exploration we combine Diagram 4b from Chapter 4 and Diagram 3n from Chapter 3 with the 'Greatest Name' to discover (Diagram 5j) both the scientific and the spiritual power of the Holy Spirit!

The human reality—the human spirit that acts purposefully and transforms itself and its surroundings—is represented by the central vertical portion of the divine economy model. There is transformation; and humans are spiritual beings in addition to being physical and intellectual beings. The central vertical line in the 'Greatest Name' symbolizes the Holy Spirit which connects God to mankind via the Manifestations of God. The power of the Holy Spirit is captured scientifically in the divine economy theory by simply redefining praxeology as the study of purposeful action of humans as spiritual beings.

Another way to scientifically capture the spiritual power of the Holy Spirit is to recognize that the essence of the entrepreneurial spirit is alertness. This is synonymous with the search for truth which is an inherent characteristic of human beings. It is the cause of purposeful action. The divine spark is simply a manifestation of the Holy Spirit in the lives of human beings.

Looking down at the base of the force of economic equilibrium from the fulcrum tip (Diagram 5k) we see how the divine economy theory operates as an economic equilibrium theory.

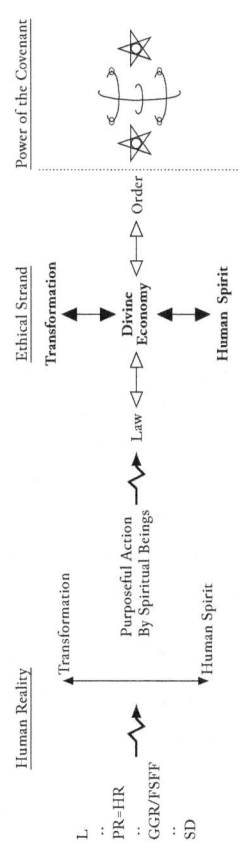

Diagram 5j: Using Science to Explore the Holy Spirit

The first thing we notice is that looking from the very specific perspective of the fulcrum tip—which represents the Justice of the Divine Economy—it lines up perfectly with the point where the Holy Spirit intersects with the Manifestation of God. This is not a coincidence. After all, the Manifestations of God are and have always been the Source of justice.

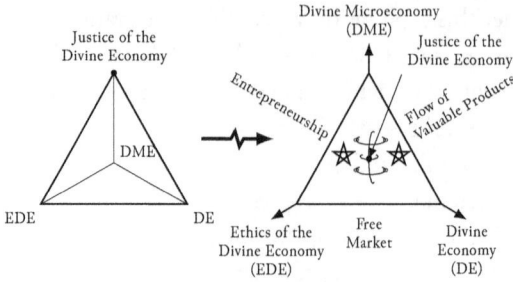

Diagram 5k: The Fulcrum Point / Intersection Point

Now let us look at some examples of how the divine economy works. Comparative advantage is an economic law which explains how it is that even if someone (or a nation) is relatively less productive in all productive activities there will be a comparative advantage in at least one productive activity. In other words, every single human being can contribute to the advancement of civilization and because they contribute productively they earn income to provide for their needs. How this economic law is possible is somewhat mind-boggling but it is true and it is undoubtedly part of God's providence.

Another supreme economic law is the disutility of labor. It drives entrepreneurship and the formation of capital. And yet humans are subjective. As you can see in Appendix A there are numerous deviations from the law of the disutility of labor due to the power of thought. [48, pp. 587–588] And so it is readily conceivable that a culture can evolve into one that regards work done to one's highest ability as equivalent to the worship of God. In other words, it is an expression of love and so humans can conquer the law of the disutility of labor if they choose to do so in a way that happens to be voluntary, thus making it perfectly compatible with the forces of equilibrium.

The entrepreneurial spirit that is in an active state is alert and ready for the transformation process. It connects itself to the flow of knowledge in an effort to seek the truth. It needs to operate in an environment of justice to function optimally; and it perceives justice within the surroundings and across time; and it renders justice by ameliorating skewed circumstances! In other words, the Holy Spirit is closely associated with the entrepreneurial spirit.

It is not coincidental that certain worldly things which are very much admired by humans are not within the realm of generation by humans. I am referring here to gold! It is true that we could allow the lower half of our dual nature to debase us, and quickly we would become a loathsome creature. The same is true with regards gold. It is not that we haven't tried to generate gold through alchemy, and in these—the Dark Ages of economics—our debasement comes as a result of our counterfeit systems of fiat currencies. If you take a step back and look at the wars and the corruptions that are caused by the violation of the economic law of a gold standard you get a glimpse of the degradation of humanity that burdens us; resulting from the violation of the gold standard. Gold can be tested for its purity, likewise, the purity of human civilization is tested by how it practices the gold standard.

Individuals are subjective which seems to make it difficult, theoretically and ethically, to give any validity to the concept of an entity at the societal level. That is not to say that there aren't countless unsubstantiated and theoretically and ethically invalid doctrines that give society a life in and of itself. Discarding these and searching for the possibility of a social expression of subjective individuals, a real possibility comes to light. The conditions are as follows: the group—that cares deeply about the affairs of the community and the concerns of the individuals in the community—consults about an issue frankly and lovingly and comes to a unanimous or a majority decision. Knowing full well that the decision may be right or it may be wrong they inform everyone about the decision. The community and the members of the elected consultative body share the conviction that only if everyone wholeheartedly supports the decision will the rightness or wrongness of the decision ever be known. If it turns out to be wrong on its own merit, not because of disruptive opposition, then the consultative process is repeated until the right decision is confirmed by real experience. If society is arranged in this manner then a group can function as a decision-maker in a manner that is compatible with the subjective nature of individuals. "A group decision, when unanimously agreed upon, may be considered as consistent as any other taken by the individual chooser in the market."[37, p. 226]

As you can tell we have been moving along the path of the divine economy into the realm of culture and order. To go further we have to look again at where we are coming from before we can decide where we want to go.

Over the ages subjective decisions were made concerning how best to achieve social cooperation. Early on these decisions were incorporated into the customs and formed the basis for the customary laws. Part of the social advancement and evolution along these lines was the codifying of the laws which facilitated the flow of knowledge. Common law was a variant of this process and actually it was a deviant, where law came under the control of the ego-driven. It is this corrupted system that is now in place.

To truly resolve this age-old problem there seems to be two primary options. Both options call for the return to codified law. In a society that rebuilds itself so that the force of economic equilibrium operates with liberty and justice there will always be a continuous refinement of the laws as a natural process. Part of the steps of refinement will be the necessity of codifying this customary law. I have two concerns about this type of codification process. First, it could succumb to corruption like it did before when it morphed into common law. And second, this continual refinement is quite a slow process which increases its vulnerability to the attacks of corruption by the ego-driven.

The other option of establishing codified law is ideal in many ways. The laws given to us by the Manifestation of God specific for the Day in which we live are codified. They are tailored especially for the needs, exigencies, and requirements of that particular Day and Age. They come from the true Source of justice and from the Law-Giver. Although implementing these laws may take time and although there will still be an ongoing discovery process for the entire Dispensation, the foundation exists immediately. If the Covenant is strong, and if it is inviolable, then there cannot be any corrupting of the codified law.

We are talking about economics, that is, the best means to attain the ends. If a Manifestation of God has given us the Laws of the Age then the best means to attain the ever-advancing civilization is to adopt these codified laws.

Assay

What we are looking for is "a system that prevents among others the gradual control of wealth in the hands of a few and the resulting state

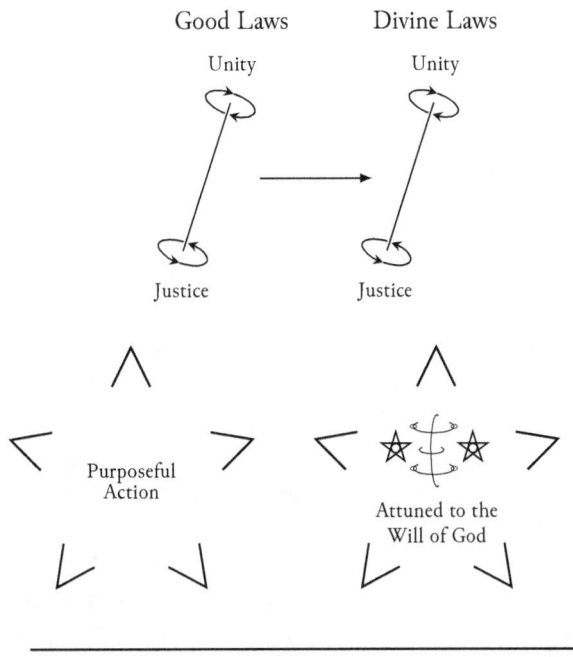

Diagram 5I: Laws and the Divine Spark

of both extremes, wealth and poverty"[8, p. 548]. In other words we want a system of liberty and justice. Science is one way to assay the true nature and value of things. Science can even be used to assay the nature and value of 'science'—as we have seen—economic science has shown that much of economics is riddled with errors and fallacies. The divine economy theory upholds and proves that the correct scientific method for economics is subjectivism. It verifies the scientific validity of classical liberalism and it verifies it as a proven system of liberty and justice.

Let's flip the coin and look at the other side! Science cannot be true science if it ignores the existence of God. In this way religion is one way to assay science. This is exactly why I developed the divine economy theory. Contemporary economics was unable to meet this test! Look at all of the discoveries that I have made this time around using the divine economy theory. More discoveries will be made in the future by future economists who use the divine economy theory. The intent of this point is to emphasize that true science and true religion go hand in hand.

Now think about how drastic the changes have to be to get from where we are to where we are going as a human civilization—to a contractual civilization made up of consultative communities. What would cause the ego-driven to change their ways? And what could possibly cause the abandonment of the ubiquitous common law? There are three major forces that can and will motivate the change. Of course there is the equilibrium force. Then there is the force of change emanating from education about the equilibrium force itself, in other words, the divine economy theory will play an important role. And then there is the fear of God. Once the Will of God for this Day is generally known there will be only a rare few, high or low alike, who will deliberately undermine their very own existence by acting in contrarian ways.

There are two dimensions to the emergence of the divine civilization embodied in the Writings of Bahá'u'lláh. The first is that the laws are clear and the Covenant is strong and inviolable. The next chapter, Chapter 6, will go on to exemplify the theoretical exposition hinted at in this chapter in the models of the Justice of the Divine Economy. It is this theoretical exposition that sets the contractual "Seal of Bahá'u'lláh" on the force that changes hearts and changes civilization. The justice in the divine economy theory relieves people of archaic religious practices that are an anathema to the ameliorating principles of classical liberalism.

The second dimension of the emergence happens to have been mentioned by Henry Hazlitt when he was envisioning the unfolding of a classical liberalism civilization: "New rules and standards must be tested by a minority before they are adopted by or enforced on everyone."[26, p. 182] Currently there is a worldwide community of individuals who are voluntarily aligning their lives according to the Laws and Teachings of Bahá'u'lláh and undergoing transformation. This minority operates completely within the Covenant and so all of the great powers described by the divine economy theory are fully available.

Two levels of testing are taking place. The Bahá'í community is facing the test of abiding by the Will of God as revealed by Bahá'u'lláh. It is through this transformative testing process that the signs of prosperity and justice will be evident for all to see. The Bahá'í community welcomes any and all critical examination of how it all works. In that way they are serving humanity—which needs to see proof before adopting change.

The second level of testing is more tragic. The equilibrium force is infinitely more powerful than any manmade ideology. Most of the institutional components and structures existing in the world today are built upon economic fallacies and other errors of human thought. The equilibrium pendulum has been pushed to its limit and will return to its point of entropy with great and cataclysmic force. The economic equilibrium and the broader equilibrium concept within the divine economy theory will be tested against the events and the trends over time. Also, the maintenance of liberty and justice—despite the world upheavals—within the stronghold of the Covenant of Bahá'u'lláh will be tested. At both levels of testing the divine economy theory and the Covenant of Bahá'u'lláh will be as a guiding light to a searching humanity.

> Logical thinking and real life are not two separate orbits. Logic is for man the only means to master the problems of reality. What is contradictory in theory, is no less contradictory in reality. No ideological inconsistency can provide a satisfactory, i.e., working, solution for the problems offered by the facts of the world. The only effect of contradictory ideologies is to conceal the real problems and thus to prevent people from finding in time an appropriate policy for solving them. Inconsistent ideologies may sometimes postpone the emergence of a manifest conflict. But they certainly aggravate the evils which they mask and render a final solution more difficult. They multiply the agonies, they intensify the hatreds, and make peaceful settlement impossible. It is a serious blunder to consider ideological contradictions harmless or even beneficial.
>
> The main objective of praxeology and economics is to substitute consistent correct ideologies for the contradictory tenets of popular eclecticism. There is no other means of preventing social disintegration and of safeguarding the steady improvement of human conditions than those provided by reason. Men must try to think through all the problems involved up to the point beyond which a human mind cannot proceed farther. They must never acquiesce in any solutions conveyed by older generations, they must always question

anew every theory and every theorem, they must never relax
in their endeavors to brush away fallacies and to find the
best possible cognition. They must fight error by unmasking
spurious doctrines and by expounding truth.[48, p. 185]

What is being sought? Justice and liberty are being sought. Law
and order are being sought. It is no longer difficult to understand that
justice is, in essence, divine. Likewise law is divine and order is divine!
Of course that means that it is beyond the conceptualization power
of human minds. It is within the domain of the Manifestations of
God. How fascinating it is to be able to see for yourself the justice and
liberty, the law and order, given to us by the Manifestation of God
known as Bahá'u'lláh!

Selected Exercises

1. When is liberty and justice closely balanced?

2. What happens to the human reality under justice?

3. Describe how reciprocity and symmetry imply justice.

4. According to divine economy theory, what is the reason that humans
   deeply value a contractual relationship?

5. Where did the ego-driven State come from?

6. What does Ludwig von Mises mean by "economics is a living thing?"

7. Use Diagram 5i to describe the influence of the Covenant of God
   on human action.

8. Discuss how the science of economics can now explore how the Holy
   Spirit influences human action.

9. What is underlying the remarkability of comparative advantage?

10. Is an economic law like the disutility of labor able to be circumvented?

11. What is the relationship between entrepreneurship and justice?

12. If the best means to attain the ends is recognizing and applying the
    Laws of Bahá'u'lláh what is the economic thing to do?

13. Is a contractual civilization made up of consultative communities the
    direction we are going? Give an example in the affirmative.

14. What is the merit of having "new rules and standards" tested by a minority before their adoption by the majority?

15. Comment on the quote of Ludwig von Mises [ref. 48, p. 185] on Pages 71 to 72 with regards the divine economy theory.

Chapter 6
Just A Step Away From Those Glorious Heights

Divine Justice and Divine Order

"Were men to strictly observe that which the Pen of the Most High hath revealed in the Crimson Book, they could then well afford to dispense with the regulations which prevail in the world. Certain exhortations have repeatedly streamed forth from the Pen of the Most High that perchance the manifestations of power and the dawning-places of might may, sometime, be enabled to enforce them."[13, p. 90]

PREAMBLE

With a foot planted firmly on the ground, the world and all of the worlds seem less daunting. Confident in the beneficence of certitude the journey embarked upon by these now fully mature individuals is like a vast ocean—constant, powerful, expansive, awesome, deep, and full of potency. On the beach where the waves continually spread themselves outwards, these exalted aspirations can be heard: "Give me more, give me more, I want more!"

INCUBATION

Immediately, to begin we have to recognize a few things. Humans are subjective and since we are all different justice is the greatest law of God for this Day. Also, there is a difference between philosophers and those who are Spiritual Teachers (the Manifestations of God). "The Spiritual Teacher is the first to follow His own teaching; He brings down into the world of action His spiritual conceptions and ideals. His Divine thoughts are made manifest to the world. His thought is Himself, from which He is inseparable."[9, p. 18] Liberty and justice is the reality of the Manifestation of God. "The Ancient Beauty hath consented to be bound with chains that mankind may be released from its bondage, and hath accepted to be made a prisoner within this most mighty Stronghold that the whole world may attain unto true liberty. He hath drained to its dregs the cup of sorrow, that all the peoples of the earth may attain unto abiding joy, and be filled with gladness."[11, p. 99] "The essence of all that We have revealed for thee is Justice, is for man to free himself from idle fancy and imitation, discern with the eye of oneness His glorious handiwork, and look into all things with a searching eye."[13, p. 156]

It is this searching eye that both high and low can use to find the foundations of life that pertain to us as individuals and to the whole of human civilization. Consider paragraph 85 in the *Kitáb-i-Aqdas* (Most Holy Book), the Book of Laws, which makes reference to Francis Joseph, the Emperor of Austria and King of Hungary. Bahá'u'lláh reproaches him for his failure to 'take the opportunity to inquire about Bahá'u'lláh Who was at that time a prisoner in 'Akká (Acre).'[15, p. 216] "O Emperor of Austria! He Who is the Dayspring of God's Light dwelt in the prison of 'Akká at the time when thou didst set forth to visit the Aqsa Mosque. Thou passed Him by, and inquired not about Him by Whom every house is exalted and every lofty gate unlocked. We, verily, made it a place whereunto the world should turn, that they might remember Me, and yet thou hast rejected Him Who is the Object of this remembrance, when He appeared with the Kingdom of God, thy Lord and the Lord of the worlds. We have been with thee at all times, and found thee clinging unto the Branch and heedless of the Root. Thy Lord, verily, is a witness unto what I say. We grieved to see thee circle round Our Name, whilst unaware of Us, though We were before thy face. Open thine eyes, that thou mayest behold this glorious Vision, and recognize Him Whom thou invokest in the daytime and in the night season, and gaze on the Light that shineth above this luminous Horizon."[15, p. 50]

"He Who is the Eternal Truth—exalted be His glory—hath made the fulfilment of every undertaking on earth dependent on material means."[12, #34] We are subjective beings interested in our own well-being and so the potential to acquire wealth motivates us to act simply out of self interest and yet wealth is of great benefit to everyone. Bahá'u'lláh then goes on to say: "Hence it is enjoined upon every individual to offer that which is the Right of God." The Right of God helps the Bahá'ís to see wealth also as a means for acting in the interest of others. Here is paragraph 97 in the *Kitáb-i-Aqdas*: "Should anyone acquire one hundred mithqáls of gold, nineteen mithqáls thereof are God's and to be rendered unto Him, the Fashioner of earth and heaven. Take heed, O people, lest ye deprive yourselves of so great a bounty. This We have commanded you, though We are well able to dispense with you and with all who are in the heavens and on earth; in it there are benefits and wisdoms beyond the ken of anyone but God, the Omniscient, the All-Informed. Say: By this means He hath desired to purify what ye possess and to enable you to draw nigh unto such stations as none can comprehend save those whom God hath willed. He, in truth, is the Beneficent, the Gracious, the Bountiful. O people! Deal not faithlessly with the Right of God, nor, without His leave, make free with its disposal. Thus hath His commandment been established in the holy Tablets, and in this exalted Book. He who dealeth faithlessly with God shall in justice meet with faithlessness himself; he, however, who acteth in accordance with God's bidding shall receive a blessing from the heaven of the bounty of his Lord, the Gracious, the Bestower, the Generous, the Ancient of Days. He, verily, hath willed for you that which is yet beyond your knowledge, but which shall be known to you when, after this fleeting life, your souls soar heavenwards and the trappings of your earthly joys are folded up. Thus admonisheth you He in Whose possession is the Guarded Tablet."[15, p. 55] Note #125 describes it further: "This verse establishes Ḥuqúqu'lláh, the Right of God, the offering of a fixed portion of the value of the believer's possessions. This offering was made to Bahá'u'lláh as the Manifestation of God and then, following His Ascension, to 'Abdu'l-Bahá as the Centre of the Covenant. In His *Will and Testament*, 'Abdu'l-Bahá provided that the Ḥuqúqu'lláh was to be offered "through the Guardian of the Cause of God". There now being no Guardian, it is offered through the Universal House of Justice as the Head of the Faith. This fund is used for the promotion of the Faith of God and its interests as well as for various philanthropic purposes."[15, p. 218]

Unlike in the past, in the *Kitáb-i-Aqdas* there are no negative assessments assigned to profit or interest. For example, "Many people stand in need of this. Because if there were no prospect for gaining interest, the affairs of men would suffer collapse or dislocation. One can seldom find a person who would manifest such consideration towards his fellow-man, his countryman or towards his own brother and would show such tender solicitude for him as to be well-disposed to grant him a loan on benevolent terms. Therefore as a token of favour towards men We have prescribed that interest on money should be treated like other business transactions that are current amongst men. Thus, now that this lucid commandment hath descended from the heaven of the Will of God, it is lawful and proper to charge interest on money, that the people of the world may, in a spirit of amity and fellowship and with joy and gladness, devotedly engage themselves in magnifying the Name of Him Who is the Well-Beloved of all mankind. Verily He ordaineth according to His Own choosing. He hath now made interest on money lawful, even as He had made it unlawful in the past."[13, p. 132] As an economist in the classical liberalism tradition I see this as an indication that free banking is a very important component of a divine economy since it has the merits of self-regulation, and since it serves the people by providing the storehouses for capital. This is in contrast to the corrupt current banking practices which mask the insolvencies of banks and promulgate a system of capital consumption and wealth redistribution.

Wealth is supposed to be protected so it can serve as capital to do the work of the world and so it can be bestowed on one's loved ones. Paragraph 109 begins with this sentence: "Unto everyone hath been enjoined the writing of a will."[15, p. 59] Note #136 further explains this: "According to the Teachings of Bahá'u'lláh, the individual has a duty to write a will and testament, and is free to dispose of his estate in whatever manner he chooses." "Bahá'u'lláh affirms that in drawing up his will 'a person hath full jurisdiction over his property', since God has permitted the individual 'to deal with that which He hath bestowed upon him in whatever manner he may desire.'"[15, p. 223]

If an individual does not have a will at the time of passing then the law of Bahá'u'lláh apportions the inheritance in a way that is beneficial to the family members, the teachers and possibly to the Houses of Justice. The first of many laws pertaining to inheritance and the will is paragraph 20: "We have divided inheritance into seven categories: to the children, We have allotted nine parts comprising five hundred and forty shares; to the wife, eight parts comprising four hundred and eighty shares; to the father, seven parts comprising four hundred and twenty shares; to the mother, six parts comprising three hundred and sixty shares; to the brothers, five parts or three hundred shares; to the sisters, four parts or two hundred and forty shares; and to the teachers, three parts or one hundred and eighty shares. Such was the ordinance of My Forerunner, He Who extolleth My Name in the night season and at the break of day. When We heard the clamour of the children as yet unborn, We doubled their share and decreased those of the rest. He, of a truth, hath power to ordain whatsoever He desireth, and He doeth as He pleaseth by virtue of His sovereign might."[15, p. 26]

It is the right of the individual property owner to do what he or she pleases with that property. In paragraph 61 Bahá'u'lláh says: "God hath bidden you to show forth kindliness towards My kindred, but He hath granted them no right to the property of others. He, verily, is self-sufficient, above any need of His creatures."[15, p. 41] In other words, an important feature of the new divine economy ethic is the traditional classical liberalism property rights ethic plus the fear of God.

Although I will come back to this later in the chapter it is time to describe the Houses of Justice since the Right of God is given to the Universal House of Justice and since inheritance sometimes is allocated to the Houses of Justice. Bahá'u'lláh makes first mention in the *Kitáb-i-Aqdas* of the Houses of Justice in paragraph 21: "Should the deceased leave no offspring, their share shall revert to the House of Justice, to be expended by the Trustees of the All-Merciful on the orphaned and widowed, and on whatsoever will bring benefit to the generality of the people, that all may give thanks unto their Lord, the All-Gracious, the Pardoner."[15, pp. 26–27] There is no welfare State in this divine system but those who are in need will be provided for. No individual will be lost because there will be a House of Justice in every city and village as described in paragraph 30: "The Lord hath ordained that in every city a House of Justice be established wherein shall gather counselors to the number of Bahá', and should it exceed this number it doth not matter. They should consider themselves as entering the Court of the presence of God, the Exalted, the Most High, and as beholding Him Who is the Unseen. It behoveth them to be the trusted ones of the Merciful among men and to regard themselves as the guardians appointed of God for all that dwell on earth. It is incumbent upon them to take counsel together and to have regard for the interests of the servants of God, for His sake, even as they regard their own interests, and to choose that which is meet and seemly. Thus hath the Lord your God commanded you. Beware lest ye put away that which is clearly revealed in His Tablet. Fear God, O ye that perceive." [15, p. 29]

From Note #56 we find: "In one of His Tablets, ʿAbduʾl-Bahá states that 'if a person is incapable of earning a living, is stricken by dire poverty or becometh helpless, then it is incumbent on the wealthy or the Deputies to provide him with a monthly allowance for his subsistence'.... By 'Deputies' is meant the representatives of the people, that is to say the members of the House of Justice." [15, p. 192] This note is a supplement to the law given by Baháʾuʾlláh in paragraph 33: "O people of Baháʾ! It is incumbent upon each one of you to engage in some occupation—such as a craft, a trade or the like. We have exalted your engagement in such work to the rank of worship of the one true God. Reflect, O people, on the grace and blessings of your Lord, and yield Him thanks at eventide and dawn. Waste not your hours in idleness and sloth, but occupy yourselves with what will profit you and others. Thus hath it been decreed in this Tablet from whose horizon hath shone the day-star of wisdom and utterance. The most despised of men in the sight of God are they who sit and beg. Hold ye fast unto the cord of means and place your trust in God, the Provider of all means." [15, p. 30] Shoghi Effendi goes on to further explain this law: "In response to a question concerning whether Baháʾuʾlláh's injunction requires a wife and mother, as well as her husband, to work for a livelihood, the Universal House of Justice has explained that Baháʾuʾlláh's directive is for the friends to be engaged in an occupation which will profit themselves and others, and that homemaking is a highly honourable and responsible work of fundamental importance to society." [15, p. 193]

Societal transformation is part of the change and two of the most dramatic changes are intimately connected to economic behavior. Benefits from cooperation will come to be very much understood. For instance, as a result of the sum total of positive societal transformations the time preference for everyone will lower, which is especially good news for people along the margin of criminal behavior. A generally lower time preference and an affinity for social cooperation will significantly decrease the desire to commit a crime.

Those who are beyond the margin are in need of greater measures to train them, if trainable. Levying fines to compensate the victims is one measure, as in paragraph 188: "Should anyone unintentionally take another's life, it is incumbent upon him to render to the family of the deceased an indemnity of one hundred mithqáls of gold. Observe ye that which hath been enjoined upon you in this Tablet, and be not of those who overstep its limits."[15, p. 87] Whereas a deliberate murder is so uncivilized that it may require the harshest of punishment as is demonstrated in paragraph 62: "Should anyone intentionally destroy a house by fire, him also shall ye burn; should anyone deliberately take another's life, him also shall ye put to death. Take ye hold of the precepts of God with all your strength and power, and abandon the ways of the ignorant. Should ye condemn the arsonist and the murderer to life imprisonment, it would be permissible according to the provisions of the Book. He, verily, hath power to ordain whatsoever He pleaseth."[15, p. 40]

Criminals beyond the margin who violate property rights may or may not be able to reform but only the most heinous will feel the full effects of the law in paragraph 45: "Exile and imprisonment are decreed for the thief, and, on the third offence, place ye a mark upon his brow so that, thus identified, he may not be accepted in the cities of God and His countries. Beware lest, through compassion, ye neglect to carry out the statutes of the religion of God; do that which hath been bidden you by Him Who is compassionate and merciful. We school you with the rod of wisdom and laws, like unto the father who educateth his son, and this for naught but the protection of your own selves and the elevation of your stations. By My life, were ye to discover what We have desired for you in revealing Our holy laws, ye would offer up your very souls for this sacred, this mighty, and most exalted Faith."[15, pp. 35–36] Note #70 explains the degree of penalty: "Bahá'u'lláh states that the determination of the degree of penalty, in accordance with the seriousness of the offence, rests with the House of Justice. The punishments for theft are intended for a future condition of society, when they will be supplemented and applied by the Universal House of Justice."[15, p. 198] Note #71 describes the mark on the forehead: "The mark to be placed on the thief's forehead serves the purpose of warning people of his proclivities. All details concerning the nature of the mark, how the mark is to be applied, how long it must be worn, on what conditions it may be removed, as well as the seriousness of various degrees of theft have been left by Bahá'u'lláh for the Universal House of Justice to determine when the law is applied."[15, p. 198]

It is obvious to most people that there are significant social costs and harm done by acts of crime but there are also social costs and harm done by acts of immorality. Fines serve as a deterrent which may be necessary for a person with a weak character to change their behavior. The fines may be less of a deterrent than the shame. Both the fines and the shame increase as described in paragraph 49: "God hath imposed a fine on every adulterer and adulteress, to be paid to the House of Justice: nine mithqáls of gold, to be doubled if they should repeat the offence. Such is the penalty which He Who is the Lord of Names hath assigned them in this world; and in the world to come He hath ordained for them a humiliating torment. Should anyone be afflicted by a sin, it behoveth him to repent thereof and return unto his Lord. He, verily, granteth forgiveness unto whomsoever He willeth, and none may question that which it pleaseth Him to ordain. He is, in truth, the Ever-Forgiving, the Almighty, the All-Praised."[15, p. 37] In Note #77 the House of Justice referred to is the Local House of Justice: "In one of His Tablets, 'Abdu'l-Bahá refers to some of the spiritual and social implications of the violation of the laws of morality and, concerning the penalty here described, He indicates that the aim of this law is to make clear to all that such an action is shameful in the eyes of God and that, in the event that the offence can be established and the fine imposed, the principal purpose is the exposure of the offenders—that they are shamed and disgraced in the eyes of society. He affirms that such exposure is in itself the greatest punishment."[15, p. 200] And in Note #78 it states: "The weight of nine of these mithqáls equals 32.775 grammes or 1.05374 troy ounces."[15, p. 201]

Other resources, too, will be available to the Houses of Justice—voluntarily—contributions and Zakat (tithe). "Full development of the institution of Zakat has fallen to the Universal House of Justice which will in the future legislate upon the details necessary for the assessment of Zakat and the operation of this institution within the guidelines provided by Bahá'u'lláh and 'Abdu'l-Bahá."[15, p. 169] The point being that a system is in the world for all to see. "Anticipating the System which the irresistible power of His Law was destined to unfold in a later age, He (Bahá'u'lláh) writes: 'The world's equilibrium hath been upset through the vibrating influence of this most great, this new World Order. Mankind's ordered life hath been revolutionized through the agency of this unique, this wondrous System—the like of which mortal eyes have never witnessed.' 'The Hand of Omnipotence hath established His Revelation upon an unassailable, an enduring foundation. Storms of human strife are powerless to undermine its basis, nor will men's fanciful theories succeed in damaging its structure.'"[21, p. 109]

The following counsel of justice is given by Bahá'u'lláh in paragraph 189: "O members of parliaments throughout the world! Select ye a single language for the use of all on earth, and adopt ye likewise a common script. God, verily, maketh plain for you that which shall profit you and enable you to be independent of others. He, of a truth, is the Most Bountiful, the All-Knowing, the All-Informed. This will be the cause of unity, could ye but comprehend it, and the greatest instrument for promoting harmony and civilization, would that ye might understand! We have appointed two signs for the coming of age of the human race: the first, which is the most firm foundation, We have set down in other of Our Tablets, while the second hath been revealed in this wondrous Book."[15, p. 88] If we go to the first ⅓ of Note #194 we find further clarification: "The first sign of the coming of age of humanity referred to in the Writings of Bahá'u'lláh is the **emergence of a science** which is described as that '**divine philosophy**' which will include the discovery of a radical approach to the **transmutation of elements**. This is an indication of the splendours of **the future stupendous expansion of knowledge**."[15, p. 250]

I find in these words given in Note #194 a remarkable parallel with the divine economy theory. First of all '**emergence of a science**' is exactly what has happened—the divine economy theory—similar to the science that emerged from Thomas Aquinas and the Spanish Scholastics during the early years of classical liberalism. Just like the philosophy of science back then, the divine economy theory can now be described as a '**divine philosophy**.' One of the features of this book that you are reading right now is the expansion of the concept of economic equilibrium to the realm of law. The concept expanded from economics to ethics to law and ultimately to what is referred to as the human civilization equilibrium which encompasses all of the sciences, each of which in some way embodies the concept of equilibrium. With this in place the '**transmutation of elements**' (all of the sciences) and the '**future stupendous expansion of knowledge**' is assured. In other words, God is the heart and soul of all knowledge.

We can now re-examine the Justice/Unity axis of the divine economy model. Remember that this is a shorthand version of the divine economy theory which contains within it the divine microeconomy theory and the divine spark. Also implied is the interconnectedness of the economy with ethics, and its transformative process towards a divine civilization, that unfolds under the influence of the elements of human civilization and the Covenant.

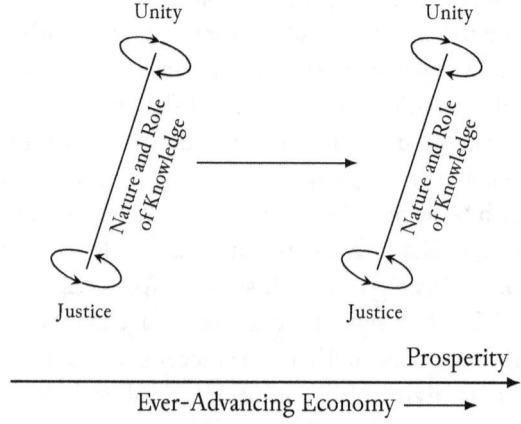

Diagram 6a: The Future Stupendous Expansion of Knowledge

Now think about this diagram in terms of paragraph 189 in the *Kitáb-i-Aqdas*. The divine justice of the counsel given by Bahá'u'lláh 'will be the cause of unity' and 'the greatest instrument for promoting harmony and civilization.' Notice the 'Nature and Role of Knowledge' axis and how it links justice to unity and how it advances as it moves to the right. According to Note #194: "This is an indication of the splendours of the future **stupendous expansion of knowledge**."

To some degree, I feel certain that the divine economy theory contributes to the emergence of a science which is described as a 'divine philosophy.'

The second ⅓ (not yet examined) of Note #194 goes on to describe the 'signs for the coming of age of the human race.' "Concerning the 'second' sign which Bahá'u'lláh indicates to have been revealed in the *Kitáb-i-Aqdas*, Shoghi Effendi states that Bahá'u'lláh, ". . . in His Most Holy Book, has enjoined the selection of a single language and the adoption of a common script for all on earth to use, an injunction which, when carried out, would, as He Himself affirms in that Book, be one of the signs of the 'coming of age of the human race.'"

Further insight into this process of mankind's coming of age and proceeding to maturity is provided by the following statement of Bahá'u'lláh: "One of the signs of the maturity of the world is that no one will accept to bear the weight of kingship. Kingship will remain with none willing to bear alone its weight. That day will be the day whereon wisdom will be manifested among mankind." [15, p. 251]

This shows the high sense of justice in the future. Kings will find that the need for consultation with their subjects is so great and that the need for exceptional nobility is so great that it is not possible to be a king under such a high standard of justice.

Again refer to Diagram 6a. The movement of the 'Nature and Role of Knowledge' axis when the human race comes of age visually complements what is the final ⅓ of Note #194: "The coming of age of the human race has been associated by Shoghi Effendi with the unification of the whole of mankind, the establishment of a world commonwealth, and an unprecedented stimulus to 'the intellectual, the moral and spiritual life of the entire human race.'"

As you can see we have gotten to the point where it is time to examine the divine order brought by Bahá'u'lláh. The laws of Bahá'u'lláh establishes and limits the Administrative Order which allows for the ethics of humankind to evolve from one stage to the next—like the ecological concept of the succession of communities—as the process of the ever-advancing civilization proceeds organically and naturally as part of the omnipresent and omniscient equilibrium force of God.

TABERNACLE

Yet, undeniably, we must go from chaos to order. Is this not what is promised in the Covenant of God? "Verily, the mission of all the prophets, the relation of all the scriptures, the diffusion of the instructions of God and the descent of His law, were all in order to establish agreement and union and to strengthen love and harmony among nations of different customs and thoughts, of diverse beliefs, doctrines, rites and habits; of various classes, tribes and races."[4, p. 596] It is through the revealed observances and laws provided via the Manifestations of God that the world is set in order. The *Kitáb-i-Aqdas* is "the chief depository wherein are enshrined those priceless elements of that Divine Civilization, the establishment of which is the primary mission of the Bahá'í Faith."[21, p. 3]

The embryonic Administrative Order, as it expands and consolidates itself within the shelter of an inviolable Covenant, will stimulate individual action within a pattern designed by Bahá'u'lláh. This is providential because: "For man's knowledge of God cannot develop fully and adequately save by observing whatsoever hath been ordained by Him and is set forth in His heavenly Book."[13, p. 267] After all, "The supreme cause for creating the world and all that is therein is for man to know God."[13, p. 267]

Human development and consequently the development of human civilization is contingent upon at least some of the people on Earth putting into effect the guidance provided by Bahá'u'lláh. "For Bahá'u'lláh, we should readily recognize, has not only imbued mankind with a new and regenerating Spirit. He has not merely enunciated certain universal principles, or propounded a particular philosophy, however potent, sound and universal these may be. In addition to these He, as well as 'Abdu'l-Bahá after Him, has, unlike the Dispensations of the past, clearly and specifically laid down a set of Laws, established definite institutions, and provided for the essentials of a Divine Economy. These are destined to be a pattern for future society, a supreme instrument for the establishment of the Most Great Peace, and the one agency for the unification of the world, and the proclamation of the reign of righteousness and justice upon the earth. Not only have they revealed all the directions required for the practical realization of those ideals which the Prophets of God have visualized, and which from time immemorial have inflamed the imagination of seers and poets in every age. They have also, in unequivocal and emphatic language, appointed those twin institutions of the House of Justice and of the Guardianship as their chosen Successors, destined to apply the principles, promulgate the laws, protect the institutions, adapt loyally and intelligently the Faith to the requirements of progressive society, and consummate the incorruptible inheritance which the Founders of the Faith have bequeathed to the world."[21, p. 19]

Of course this divine order finds its origin in the *Kitáb-i-Aqdas*. There are twin pillars that support the mighty administrative structure of this divine order—"the institutions of the Guardianship and of the Universal House of Justice."[21, p. 147] With regards the Guardianship it is "In the verses of the *Kitáb-i-Aqdas* the implications of which clearly anticipate the institution of the Guardianship; in the explanation which 'Abdu'l-Bahá, in one of His Tablets, has given to, and the emphasis He has placed upon, the hereditary principle and the law of primogeniture as having been upheld by the Prophets of the past—in these we can discern the faint glimmerings and discover the earliest intimation of the nature and working of the Administrative Order which the Will of 'Abdu'l-Bahá was at a later time destined to proclaim and formally establish."[21, p. 147] And so now we know what constitutes the basis of the divine order—the *Kitáb-i-Aqdas* and the *Will and Testament of 'Abdu'l-Bahá*.

"These twin institutions of the Administrative Order of Bahá'u'lláh should be regarded as divine in origin, essential in their functions and complementary in their aim and purpose. Their common, their fundamental object is to insure the continuity of that divinely-appointed authority which flows from the Source of our Faith, to safeguard the unity of its followers and to maintain the integrity and flexibility of its teachings."[21, p. 148] "Divorced from the institution of the Guardianship the World Order of Bahá'u'lláh would be mutilated and permanently deprived of that hereditary principle which, as 'Abdu'l-Bahá has written, has been invariably upheld by the Law of God."[21, p. 148] "Severed from the no less essential institution of the Universal House of Justice this same System of the Will of 'Abdu'l-Bahá would be paralyzed in its action and would be powerless to fill in those gaps which the Author of the *Kitáb-i-Aqdas* has deliberately left in the body of His legislative and administrative ordinances."[21, p. 148]

From the *Will and Testament of 'Abdu'l-Bahá* we read these emphatic words; "The sacred and youthful branch, the Guardian of the Cause of God, as well as the Universal House of Justice to be universally elected and established, are both under the care and protection of the Abha Beauty, under the shelter and unerring guidance of the Exalted One (may my life be offered up for them both). Whatsoever they decide is of God."[3, p. 11] Shoghi Effendi goes on to explain: "From these statements it is made indubitably clear and evident that the Guardian of the Faith has been made the Interpreter of the Word and that the Universal House of Justice has been invested with the function of legislating on matters not expressly revealed in the teachings. The interpretation of the Guardian, functioning within his own sphere, is as authoritative and binding as the enactments of the International House of Justice, whose exclusive right and prerogative is to pronounce upon and deliver the final judgment on such laws and ordinances as Bahá'u'lláh has not expressly revealed. Neither can, nor will ever, infringe upon the sacred and prescribed domain of the other. Neither will seek to curtail the specific and undoubted authority with which both have been divinely invested."[21, p. 149]

It may be a little difficult for a disinterested observer, so early on, to appreciate the importance or the scope of the Administrative Order that is being practiced by the worldwide Bahá'í community. "Let no one, while this System is still in its infancy, misconceive its character, belittle its significance or misrepresent its purpose. The bedrock on which this Administrative Order is founded is God's immutable Purpose for mankind in this day. The Source from which it derives its inspiration is no one less than Bahá'u'lláh Himself."[21, p. 156]

If you visualize (Diagram 6b) a rotating axis similar to the Justice/Unity axis in the divine economy model then ponder the following analogy: "The axis round which its institutions revolve are the authentic provisions of the *Will and Testament of 'Abdu'l-Bahá*. Its guiding principles are the truths which He Who is the unerring Interpreter of the teachings of our Faith has so clearly enunciated in His public addresses throughout the West. The laws that govern its operation and limit its functions are those which have been expressly ordained in the *Kitáb-i-Aqdas*."[21, p. 156]

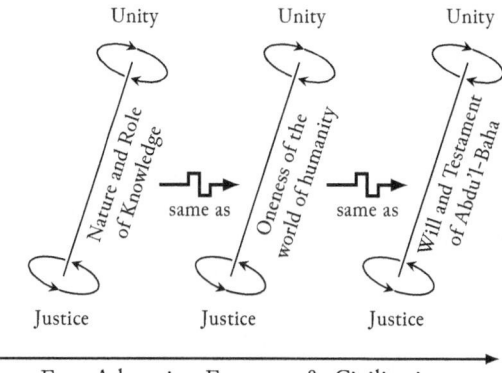

Ever-Advancing Economy & Civilization

Diagram 6b: The Axis of Oneness of the World of Humanity is the Power of the Covenant

The structure of this divine order culminates in a divine civilization with a divine economy. "The pillars that sustain its authority and buttress its structure are the twin institutions of the Guardianship and of the Universal House of Justice. The central, the underlying aim which animates it is the establishment of the New World Order as adumbrated by Bahá'u'lláh."[21, p. 156] This culmination is what was first portrayed in the Complete Model of the Divine Economy Over Time (Diagram 3h) and further illustrated in the Complete Model of the Justice of the Divine Economy (Diagram 3v).

Put into the context of classical liberalism with an appreciation of Aristotelian philosophy Shoghi Effendi captures the essence of these twin institutions: "The hereditary authority which the Guardian is called upon to exercise, the vital and essential functions which the Universal House of Justice discharges, the specific provisions requiring its democratic election by the representatives of the faithful—these combine to demonstrate the truth that this divinely revealed Order, which can never be identified with any of the standard types of government referred to by Aristotle in his works, embodies and blends with the spiritual verities on which it is based the beneficent elements which are to be found in each one of them."[21, p. 154]

The House of Justice is really like one institution at three levels. "The House of Justice is an institution created by Bahá'u'lláh. He refers to two levels of this institution: the Local Houses of Justice, responsible for each town or village, and the Universal House of Justice. ʿAbdu'l-Bahá, in His *Will and Testament*, added an intermediate level, the Secondary Houses of Justice. It is only on the Universal House of Justice that infallibility has been conferred. At the present time, to stress their purely spiritual functions, the Local and Secondary Houses of Justice are designated Local and National Spiritual Assemblies."[6, p. 172] "The importance, nay the absolute necessity of these local Assemblies is manifest when we realize that in the days to come they will evolve into the local Houses of Justice, and at present provide the firm foundation on which the structure of the Master's Will is to be reared in future."[20, p. 37] "They will be empowered, in such matters as marriage, divorce, and inheritance, to execute and apply, within their respective jurisdictions, and with the sanction of civil authorities, such laws and ordinances as have been expressly provided in their Most Holy Book."[21, p. 200]

Also in every city a Local Spiritual Assembly (which will in due time evolve into a local House of Justice) is prayerfully elected every year and that body of nine individuals takes counsel together "to choose that which is meet and seemly."[15, p. 29] The measure of that which is meet and seemly is the principle of divine justice which is "the crowning distinction of all Local and National Assemblies, in their capacity as forerunners of the Universal House of Justice."[22, p. 27] "The purpose of justice is the appearance of unity among men... The organization of the world and the tranquillity of mankind depend upon it."[22, p. 28]

One of the primary skills needed, developed, and used in the Houses of Justice and throughout the whole of the Baháʾí community life is consultation. "Baháʾuʾlláh has established consultation as one of the fundamental principles of His Faith and has exhorted the believers to 'take counsel together in all matters. He describes consultation as 'the lamp of guidance which leadeth the way' and as 'the bestower of understanding'."[15, p. 190] This is a sound method for combining wisdom and discovery. "The unfettered freedom of the individual should be tempered with mutual consultation and sacrifice, and the spirit of initiative and enterprise should be reinforced by a deeper realization of the supreme necessity for concerted action and a fuller devotion to the common weal."[20, p. 87]

And now we will consider the most democratic system (without the evils inherent in manmade democratic systems) ever known or expressed by humankind—that is—besides the market. It is called the Nineteen Day Feast. Once every Bahá'í month (there are nineteen days in each month in a Bahá'í calendar) the community gathers together for prayers, consultation and fellowship. At the Feast the individuals consult among themselves and also with the institution of the local Spiritual Assembly, offering suggestions and recommendations to the Assembly for further consultation by them. "'Abdu'l-Bahá and Shoghi Effendi after Him have gradually unfolded the institutional significance of this injunction. 'Abdu'l-Bahá emphasized the importance of the spiritual and devotional character of these gatherings. Shoghi Effendi, besides further elaborating the devotional and social aspects of the Feast, has developed the administrative element of such gatherings and, in systematically instituting the Feast, has provided for a period of consultation on the affairs of the Bahá'í community, including the sharing of news and messages."[15, p. 202]

The beauty of such an organic and divine system is its flexibility combined with its rock-solid stability. The system of Bahá'u'lláh "will, as its component parts, its organic institutions, begin to function with efficiency and vigor, assert its claim and demonstrate its capacity to be regarded not only as the nucleus but the very pattern of the New World Order destined to embrace in the fullness of time the whole of mankind."[21, p. 144]

Who can deny what all of us see? "As we view the world around us, we are compelled to observe the manifold evidences of that universal fermentation which, in every continent of the globe and in every department of human life, be it religious, social, economic or political, is purging and reshaping humanity in anticipation of the Day when the wholeness of the human race will have been recognized and its unity established. A twofold process, however, can be distinguished, each tending, in its own way and with an accelerated momentum, to bring to a climax the forces that are transforming the face of our planet. The first is essentially an integrating process, while the second is fundamentally disruptive. The former, as it steadily evolves, unfolds a System which may well serve as a pattern for that world polity towards which a strangely-disordered world is continually advancing; while the latter, as its disintegrating influence deepens, tends to tear down, with increasing violence, the antiquated barriers that seek to block humanity's progress towards its destined goal. The constructive process stands associated with the nascent Faith of Bahá'u'lláh, and is the harbinger of the New World Order that Faith must erelong establish. The destructive forces that characterize the other should be identified with a civilization that has refused to answer to the expectation of a new age, and is consequently falling into chaos and decline."[21, p. 169]

And the process is ongoing and ever-changing and it requires flexibility "inasmuch as for each day there is a new problem and for every problem an expedient solution, such affairs should be referred to the Ministers of the House of Justice that they may act according to the needs and requirements of the time."[13, p. 27]

Both the Covenant and the loving counsel of Shoghi Effendi will make sure that its rock-solid stability never becomes an earthly anchor. "It is surely for those to whose hands so priceless a heritage has been committed to prayerfully watch lest the tool should supersede the Faith itself,"[21, p. 9] Shoghi Effendi goes on, "I need not dwell upon what I have already reiterated and emphasized that the administration of the Cause is to be conceived as an instrument and not a substitute for the Faith of Bahá'u'lláh, that it should be regarded as a channel through which His promised blessings may flow, that it should guard against such rigidity as would clog and fetter the liberating forces released by His Revelation."[21, p. 8]

Nothing could be more perfect than to have Shoghi Effendi, the Guardian of the Cause of God and a magnificent contributor to the classical liberalism tradition, describe the divine order that embodies the divine laws given to us by Bahá'u'lláh:

> The Bahá'í Commonwealth of the future, of which this vast Administrative Order is the sole framework, is, both in theory and practice, not only unique in the entire history of political institutions, but can find no parallel in the annals of any of the world's recognized religious systems. No form of democratic government; no system of autocracy or of dictatorship, whether monarchical or republican; no intermediary scheme of a purely aristocratic order; nor even any of the recognized types of theocracy, whether it be the Hebrew Commonwealth, or the various Christian ecclesiastical organizations, or the Imamate

or the Caliphate in Islam—none of these can be identified or be said to conform with the Administrative Order which the master-hand of its perfect Architect has fashioned.

This new-born Administrative Order incorporates within its structure certain elements which are to be found in each of the three recognized forms of secular government, without being in any sense a mere replica of any one of them, and without introducing within its machinery any of the objectionable features which they inherently possess. It blends and harmonizes, as no government fashioned by mortal hands has as yet accomplished, the salutary truths which each of these systems undoubtedly contains without vitiating the integrity of those God-given verities on which it is ultimately founded.

The Administrative Order of the Faith of Bahá'u'lláh must in no wise be regarded as purely democratic in character inasmuch as the basic assumption which requires all democracies to depend fundamentally upon getting their mandate from the people is altogether lacking in this Dispensation. In the conduct of the administrative affairs of the Faith, in the enactment of the legislation necessary to supplement the laws of the *Kitáb-i-Aqdas*, the members of the Universal House of Justice, it should be borne in mind, are not, as Bahá'u'lláh's utterances clearly imply, responsible to those whom they represent, nor are they allowed to be governed by the feelings, the general opinion, and even the convictions of the mass of the faithful, or of those who directly elect them. They are to follow, in a prayerful attitude, the dictates and promptings of their conscience. They may, indeed they must, acquaint themselves with the conditions prevailing among the community, must weigh dispassionately in their minds the merits of any case presented for their consideration, but must reserve for themselves the right of an unfettered decision. "God will verily inspire them with whatsoever He willeth," is Bahá'u'lláh's incontrovertible assurance. They, and not the body of those who either directly or indirectly elect them, have thus been made the recipients of the divine guidance which is at once the life-blood and ultimate safeguard of this Revelation. Moreover, he who symbolizes the hereditary principle in this Dispensation has been made the interpreter of the words of its Author, and ceases consequently, by virtue of the actual authority vested in him, to be the figurehead invariably associated with the prevailing systems of constitutional monarchies.

Nor can the Bahá'í Administrative Order be dismissed as a hard and rigid system of unmitigated autocracy or as an idle imitation of any form of absolutistic ecclesiastical government, whether it be the Papacy, the Imamate or any other similar institution, for the obvious reason that upon the international elected representatives of the followers of Bahá'u'lláh has been conferred the exclusive right of legislating on matters not expressly revealed in the Bahá'í writings. Neither the Guardian of the Faith nor any institution apart from the International House of Justice can ever usurp this vital and essential power or encroach upon that sacred right. The abolition of professional priesthood with its accompanying sacraments of baptism, of communion and of confession of sins, the laws requiring the election by universal suffrage of all local, national, and international Houses of Justice, the total absence of episcopal authority with its attendant privileges, corruptions and bureaucratic tendencies, are further evidences of the non-autocratic character of the Bahá'í Administrative Order and of its inclination to democratic methods in the administration of its affairs.

Nor is this Order identified with the name of Bahá'u'lláh to be confused with any system of purely aristocratic government in view of the fact that it upholds, on the one hand, the hereditary principle and entrusts the Guardian of the Faith with the obligation of interpreting its teachings, and provides, on the other, for the free and direct election from among the mass of the faithful of the body that constitutes its highest legislative organ.

Whereas this Administrative Order cannot be said to have been modeled after any of these recognized systems of government, it nevertheless embodies, reconciles and assimilates within its framework such wholesome elements as are to be found in each one of them. The hereditary authority which the Guardian is called upon to exercise, the vital and essential functions which the Universal House of Justice discharges, the specific provisions requiring its democratic election by the representatives of the faithful—these combine to demonstrate the truth that this divinely revealed Order, which can never be identified with any of the standard types of government referred to by Aristotle in his works, embodies and blends with the spiritual verities on which it is based the beneficent elements which are to be found in each one of them. The admitted evils inherent in each of these systems being rigidly and permanently excluded, this unique Order, however long it may endure and however extensive its ramifications, cannot ever degenerate into any form of despotism, of oligarchy, or of demagogy which must sooner or later corrupt the machinery of all man-made and essentially defective political institutions.[21, p. 154]

ASSAY

In all frankness, nationalism is childish! Evidence of change and decay is all around us but for some reason we expect that the existing manmade, human institutions and legal standards and political theories are sacrosanct. How foolish.

Is such foolishness good for humanity? The oneness of the logical structure of all of us binds us together and our conclusion—worldwide—is that there is and there needs to be an organic change in the structure of present-day society. This knowledge is deeper than it has ever been before and it is precisely from this kind of heartfelt experience and thought that a new civilization begins.

Let's forget childishness, what is longed for are the exalted concepts of maturity. The ideals of liberty, freedom and liberalism have spread around the world. The desire to know oneself and those things that lead to honor or abasement are permeating every society. It is essential to know "What is man?" before we can think about human government. Ultimately—and we are the fortunate ones to be alive in this Day—theocracy was the reason for creation, the purpose of God and for the creation of the human being.

But it is in our nature to say "No" and that is our right as part of our free will; which happens to be the reason why we necessarily can conclude that what the future holds can be called a voluntary theocracy! God does not want to be loved by compulsion. Those who realize that there is a source of all of the powers that are greater than themselves will investigate the existence of God, using the sciences and religion.

It has been over 1300 years since Muḥammad and over 2000 years since Jesus and so the great Mystery of a Manifestation of God is not something that is familiar to us. What probably is familiar, however, is the historical occurrence of the associated destruction of the old 'world' order (characteristic of that particular period of human history) and the consequent expanding confederations (tribe – city/state – nation, etc.) that followed Their Appearance.

Characteristic of a theocracy is the appearance of two Names of God, the "All-Pervading" (everyone benefits) and the "Educator" (people learn how to solve exigent problems). For example, mankind did not have a concept of, nor the means of, world unity until the coming of Baháʾuʾlláh in this wondrous Age. And how could that possibly be accomplished in a way that combines the best of the systems of monarchy, and elected institutions, and liberal political freedom, and additionally, without it ever degenerating?

The Word of God is the bringing together of "B" and "E" and it is! Uniquely in this Day Baháʾuʾlláh Wrote with His Own Pen and the originals are protected and incorruptible so the Word of God remains pure. Then as part of His Texts Baháʾuʾlláh appointed ʿAbduʾl-Bahá as the Center of His Covenant and as the Perfect Exemplar of the Word of God. Never in history has such a human being ever been known and so that legacy exists and it serves as a strong and enduring bedrock. And Baháʾuʾlláh Himself created the institutions of perfection, relative to the needs and exigencies (as time passes)—the Guardianship and the Universal House of Justice. Consequently there is uniquely the rock solid text; a perfect example; and flexibility in its application to the secondary affairs that change over time. The force released by the Word of God is canalized, the authority to interpret is clear, and the foundation of a divine civilization lain. Effectively, "When the love of God is established, everything else will be realized."[5, p. 238]

In the hearts the force released by the Word of God stirs the desire to know and love the lowly and suffering Manifestation of God. Despite Their power They endured cruelties so that we could bask in the Sun of God's beneficence. Institutions, relationships, peace, the establishment of unity, and human refinement—all by and through the Word of God—plus under the contractual guarantee of the Covenant that is unique to this Day; such is voluntary theocracy.

Emerging as spiritual beings from our animal roots, more constantly aware of God, and removing the barriers that prevent unity by making the Word of God the foundation of education, we approach the essential basis of theocracy: this is to know "What is being human?" Humankind is now mature enough for that reality to be made manifest;

for fulfilling God's purpose for creating the universe, and to mold our wisdom and understanding using consultation and compassion. This is what the Bahá'í community brings to the table: specifically, living within the Covenant.

Evidence shows that people are moving all around the world such that 'one human race' is becoming a priori knowledge—not requiring a second thought—setting the stage for this next development in the evolution of the principle of the oneness of humankind. The fragmented and parochial laws cannot suffice. Appropriately, law is what God delivers to us through His Manifestation. "The Laws of God are not imposition of will, or of power, or pleasure, but the resolutions of truth, reason and justice."[9, p. 154] Impelled by the spirit of the age and the needs of the times we voluntarily choose theocracy. "Does not the very operation of the world-unifying forces that are at work in this age necessitate that He Who is the Bearer of the Message of God in this day should not only reaffirm that self-same exalted standard of individual conduct inculcated by the Prophets gone before Him, but embody in His appeal, to all governments and peoples, the essentials of that social code, that Divine Economy, which must guide humanity's concerted efforts in establishing that all-embracing federation which is to signalize the advent of the Kingdom of God on this earth?"[21, p. 60] Yes indeed!

Selected Exercises

1. How favorable to economic advancement is prescribing that interest on money be "treated like other business transactions?"

2. Does acknowledging that "a person has full jurisdiction over his property" match with the philosophy of classical liberalism?

3. Will the orphaned and widowed and those in need find relief even though there is no welfare State, and what role does the House of Justice play?

4. Does the injunction to engage in some kind of occupation include homemaking?

5. How do the laws of God protect property rights, even from those who refuse to reform themselves?

6. Describe how laws serve as a disincentive to criminality and immorality and at the same time provide resources for those who are in need of assistance.

7. Who would have thought it possible to have voluntary taxation! Explain as best you can how Zakat is a form of voluntary taxation that increases the resources to be used to bring benefit to the generality of the people.

8. To you, is the divine economy theory an example of an "emergence of a science" and why?

9. Compare the divine economy theory as a divine philosophy with the philosophy of classical liberalism.

10. Describe how all sciences have the concept of equilibrium and that the identification of God as the force behind the equilibrium brings to the surface the idea of the "transmutation of elements."

11. Referring to Diagram 6a describe the unprecedented stimulus to "the intellectual, the moral and spiritual life of the entire human race."

12. Is there any reason not to consider the pattern for future society given by Bahá'u'lláh?

13. What constitutes the basis of the divine order of Bahá'u'lláh?

14. What are the twin institutions that serve as pillars?

15. Describe the relationship between consultation and justice.

16. Considering social cooperation as an ultimate end, comment on quote [ref. 20, p. 87] on Page 90.

17. Why is the Nineteen Day Feast one of the most democratic systems ever known?

18. What features make the Administrative Order of Bahá'u'lláh flexible over time?

19. Find at least one of the "Ten Principles of Classical Liberalism" from Chapter 4 in quote [ref. 21, p. 154] on Pages 92 to 95.

Epilogue

"The body of economic knowledge is an essential element in the structure of human civilization; it is the foundation upon which modern industrialism and all the moral, intellectual, technological, and therapeutical achievements of the last centuries have been built. It rests with men whether they will make the proper use of the rich treasure with which this knowledge provides them or whether they will leave it unused. But if they fail to take the best advantage of it and disregard its teachings and warnings, they will not annul economics; they will stamp out society and the human race." [48, p. 881]   —*Ludwig von Mises*

Maturation is the process which led us through the tumultuous adolescence of not knowing who we are. It is assumed that we now understand and appreciate human action. Without doubt **human action** is a much deeper concept than just the meaning of these two combined words!

Human action is uniquely human! Ontologically speaking, no thing above it or below it has such a compositional asset and essence. It is exalted above the mineral, the vegetable, and the animal. It has time and free will as its parameters, and so, that which is above it are also of a different nature. Only us and those who are like us have the honor of fulfilling this great station in the world of creation.

With a special power behind the joining of 'B' and 'E' together to make the word 'Be' as in 'Be and it is,' action is the very essence of what is human and so is language. The descriptive function of language releases our ability to pursue the concept of truth which leads us to discover the oneness of humankind and the seamlessness between all of the sciences and between science and religion.

Yet it would be a mistake to think that religion or these sciences are complete—because knowledge is infinite. Ours is the honor to pursue it. Divine economy theory found weaknesses in macroeconomics and microeconomics and in the link between ethics and economics and it found a very weak theoretical connection between law and economics.

Justice protects the human reality and liberty allows for the expression of the human reality. In an environment of liberty and justice the ultimate end of social cooperation is attained again and again as part of the process of an ever-advancing civilization (Diagrams E1 to E3).

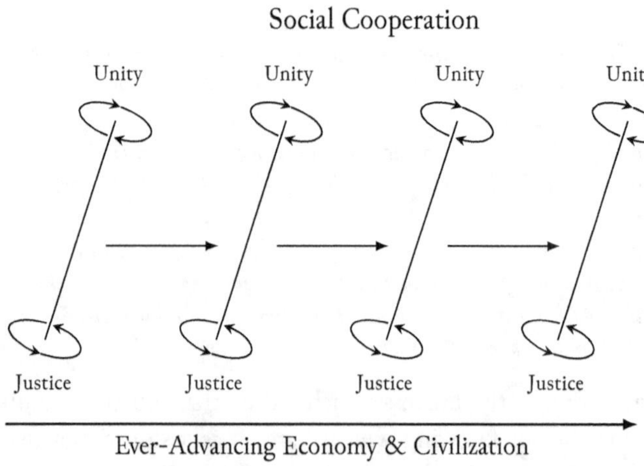

Social Cooperation

Diagram E1: Ever-Evolving Social Cooperation

The spiritualization of this process cannot be disregarded because love is an exponential contributor to true human cooperation. In fact it is the essential ingredient in the inner workings of unity (Diagram E2).

At some point unity comes to fruition as a new stage of social cooperation which then initiates a new degree of maturation within the domain of justice (Diagram E3). The unity consequently shining from this whole dynamic is a fundamental and foundational element in the process of the ever-advancing civilization.

Peace and prosperity are imminent. "A higher standard of living also brings about a higher standard of culture and civilization."[50, pp. 89–90]

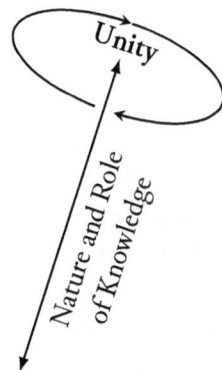

Diagram E2: Inner Workings of Unity

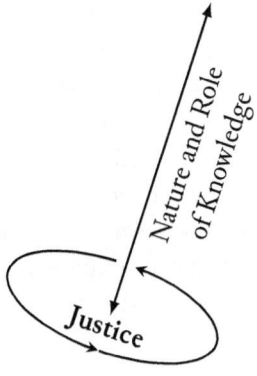

Diagram E3: Initiating the Domain of Justice

Each step along the way raises the capacity of the population to take charge of its own spiritual, social, and intellectual development.

Divine economy theory has a role to play in the spiritual, social, and intellectual development of individuals for many reasons. First of all, it is comprehensive of all disciplines from its very beginning to its end. It is all about creating an environment of liberty and justice so that the flow of knowledge is always at its maximum. "It is essential that scholars and the spiritually learned should undertake in all sincerity and purity of intent and for the sake of God alone, to counsel and exhort the masses and clarify their vision with that collyrium which is knowledge."[7, p. 39]

But human knowledge cannot ever ascend past the concept of time. It is bound to time. To gain knowledge beyond this realm requires an Alpha and an Omega! The knowledge given to the Manifestations of God transcends time. Using the divine economy theory it is possible to appreciate Their contributions to the story of human evolution.

At this stage of maturity the Bahá'ís are "learning to apply the Teachings to achieve progress," and this "could be taken as the very definition of Bahá'í social and economic development."[36, p. 128] The Revelation of Bahá'u'lláh can also be used to test the divine economy theory. In the human sciences this is one of the great values of the Manifestation of God for each Day—to test the sciences and to inspire the sciences.

The Word of God given to us by Bahá'u'lláh is pure and vast. The Covenant of God given to us by Bahá'u'lláh is inviolable. These may seem like they are only important to religion, but—lest we forget the seamlessness between science and religion—that would not be correct. What this purity and inviolability means is that all ego-driven interpretation and all ego-driven intervention are now abolished. Gone with them will be the social diseases that they cause. Over time societies will vie with each other to eliminate the State, fully confident in the divine law and the divine order of Bahá'u'lláh.

Appendix A

XXI. WORK AND WAGES

From Ludwig von Mises, *Human Action*, The Fourth Edition, (Irvington-on-Hudson, NY: Foundation for Economic Education, 1996), p. 587–8.

1. Introversive Labor and Extroversive Labor

A man may overcome the disutility of labor (forego the enjoyment of leisure) for various reasons.

1. He may work in order to make his mind and body strong, vigorous, and agile. The disutility of labor is not a price expended for the attainment of these goals; overcoming it is inseparable from the contentment sought. The most conspicuous examples are genuine sport, practiced without any design for reward and social success, and the search for truth and knowledge pursued for its own sake and not as a means of improving one's own efficiency and skill in the performance of other kinds of labor aiming at other ends.[1]

2. He may submit to the disutility of labor in order to serve God. He sacrifices leisure to please God and to be rewarded in the beyond by eternal bliss and in the earthly pilgrimage by the supreme delight which the certainty of having complied with all religious duties affords. (If, however, he serves God in order to attain worldly ends—his daily

---

1. Cognition does not aim at a goal beyond the act of knowing. What satisfies the thinker is thinking as such, not obtaining perfect knowledge, a goal inaccessible to man.

bread and success in his secular affairs—his conduct does not differ substantially from other endeavors to attain mundane advantages by expending labor. Whether the theory guiding his conduct is correct and whether his expectations will materialize are irrelevant to the catallactic qualification of his mode of acting.)[2]

3. He may toil in order to avoid greater mischief. He submits to the disutility of labor in order to forget, to escape from depressing thoughts and to banish annoying moods; work for him is, as it were, a perfected refinement of play. This refined playing must not be confused with the simple games of children which are merely pleasure-producing. (However, there are also other children's games. Children too are sophisticated enough to indulge in refined play.)

4. He may work because he prefers the proceeds he can earn by working to the disutility of labor and the pleasures of leisure.

The labor of the classes 1, 2, 3 is expended because the disutility of labor in itself—and not its product—satisfies. One toils and troubles not in order to reach a goal at the termination of the march, but for the very sake of marching. The mountain-climber does not want simply to reach the peak, he wants to reach it by climbing. He disdains the rack railway which would bring him to the summit more quickly and without trouble even though the fare is cheaper than the costs incurred by climbing (e.g., the guide's fee). The toil of climbing does not gratify him immediately; it involves disutility of labor. But it is precisely overcoming the disutility of labor that satisfies him. A less exerting ascent would please him not better, but less.

We may call the labor of classes 1, 2, and 3 introversive labor and distinguish it from the extroversive labor of class 4. In some cases introversive labor may bring about—as a by-product as it were —results for the attainment of which other people would submit to the disutility of labor. The devout may nurse sick people for a heavenly reward; the truth seeker, exclusively devoted to the search for knowledge, may discover a practically useful device. To this extent introversive labor may influence the supply on the market. But as a rule catallactics is concerned only with extroversive labor.

---

2. It is hardly necessary to remark that comparing the craving for knowledge and the conduct of a pious life with sport and play does not imply any disparagement of either.

The psychological problems raised by introversive labor are catallactically irrelevant. Seen from the point of view of economics introversive labor is to be qualified as consumption. Its performance as a rule requires not only the personal efforts of the individuals concerned, but also the expenditure of material factors of production and the produce of other peoples' extroversive, not immediately gratifying labor that must be bought by the payment of wages. The practice of religion requires places of worship and their equipment, sport requires diverse utensils and apparatus, trainers and coaches. All these things belong in the orbit of consumption.

Glossary

a priori: working from something that is already known or self-evident to arrive at a conclusion.

Active Entrepreneurship: a state of alertness where opportunities are easily discerned to be acted upon.

Arbiter: somebody who can settle a dispute or decide an issue.

Austrian School of Thought: refers to the Mengerian line of economics championed by Ludwig von Mises.

Authoritarian Law: law imposed by authority, accepted because of the domination by that authority.

Catallactic: those actions which are conducted on the basis of monetary calculations.

Catalyst: somebody or something that makes a change happen or brings about an event.

Coercive: using force or threats to make somebody do something against his or her will.

Collyrium: eye cleanser.

Common Law: laws set by precedence rather than by the principle of justice.

Conscientiously: doing something according to the person's sense of right and wrong.

Covenant of God: the promise in all Scriptures that God would always guide humankind.

Conveyancing: the branch of law practice consisting of examining titles, giving opinions as to their validity, and drawing of deeds for the conveyance of property from one person to another.

Customary Laws: laws that appeared in society to facilitate social cooperation.

Deductive: based on logic or reason.

Determinism: the doctrine or belief that everything, including every human act, is caused by something and that there is no real free will.

Disutility of labor: Humans prefer ease over hardship.

Divine Economy: God is the power behind the equilibrium force, which cannot be comprehended by the limited understanding of human minds, therefore all human intervention into the economy corrupts rather than improves the economy.

Divine Spark: the alertness that triggers transformation.

Ego-Driven: The delusion created by the lower nature of a human being who haughtily refuses to acknowledge the things beyond his or her comprehension.

Ends: a goal or purpose.

Episcopal: involving or recognizing church government by bishops.

Epistemological: pertaining to the nature of knowledge, in particular its foundations, scope, and validity.

Ethical Economics: recognition that ethics and economics are inseparable and that subjectivism is the proper scientific methodology enabling further study.

Federalism: a political system in which several states or regions defer some powers to a central government while retaining a certain measure of self-government.

Fractional-Reserve Banking: violating the contractual relationship by lending more money than has been deposited.

Free Enterprise: no artificial barriers, no deterrents facing any of the participants in the economy.

Human Civilization Equilibrium: the balancing force of harmony and symmetry and reciprocity underlying all things in the human sciences.

Ḥuqúqu'lláh: the Right of God.

Indemnity: protection or insurance against possible loss, damage, or liability.

Laxity: the condition or fact of being not strict or careful enough.

Legislation: the process of writing and passing laws.

Logic: the branch of philosophy that deals with the theory of deductive and inductive arguments to distinguish good from bad reasoning.

Macroeconomics: the study of the economy from a perspective of generality, as a starting point for deduction.

Manifestations of God: the Messengers of God, the Prophets of God.

Means: something that is available and makes it possible for somebody to do something.

Metaphysics: the branch of philosophy concerned with the study of the nature of being and beings, existence, time and space, and causality.

Microeconomics: the study of the economy immediately surrounding individuals.

Mixed Economy: the same as a hampered economy, an economy burdened by interventionism.

Monopoly: long-run restricted access, protected by intervention, which negatively affects production and prices.

Objective: existing independently of the individual mind or perception.

Opprobrium: scorn, contempt, or severe criticism.

Panoply: an impressive and magnificent display or array of something.

Parochial: concerned only with narrow local concerns without any regard for more general or wider issues.

Philanthropic: devoted to helping other people.

Philosophy of Classical Liberalism: the philosophical foundation underlying Austrian economics which places great value on liberty and justice.

Positivism: the theory that knowledge can be acquired only through direct observation and experimentation, and not through metaphysics or theology.

Praxeology: human action logic over time.

Precipice: a high, vertical, or very steep rock face: or a very dangerous situation.

Reciprocity: a relationship between people involving the exchange of goods, services, favors, or obligations.

Relative Morality: once severed from the ethics brought by the Manifestations of God a degenerate form of morality becomes 'normal.'

Restitution: compensation for a loss, damage, or injury.

State: A state is a territorial monopolist of compulsion, an agency which may engage in continual, institutionalized property rights violations and the exploitation of private property owners through expropriation, taxation and regulation (Hoppe).

Subjective: each person has a unique perspective and therein lies their value.

Subsidiarity: the principle that political power should be exercised by the smallest or least central unit of government.

Talismanic: something believed to have magical properties.

Theology: the study of God and religion.

Tort Law: in civil law, a wrongful act for which damages can be sought by the injured party.

Totalitarianism: relating to or operating a centralized government system in which a single party without opposition rules over political, economic, social, and cultural life.

Vestiges: a trace or sign of something that is no longer present.

Wealth Transfer Theory of Government: the practice of governments, out of ignorance of the destructiveness of interventionism, leading to the creation of two classes: the politically connected and the politically unconnected.

Western Civilization: the emergence of a highly productive civilization, due to the protection of capital and of property rights.

List of References

[1] 'Abdu'l-Bahá. *Foundations of World Unity*. US Bahá'í Publishing Trust, 1968. Fourth Printing.

[2] idem. *Bahá'í World Faith*. US Bahá'í Publishing Trust, 1968. Sixth printing of the 1956 edition.

[3] idem. *Will and Testament of 'Abdu'l-Bahá*. Bahá'í Publishing Trust, 1971.

[4] idem. *Tablets of 'Abdu'l-Bahá*. Vol. 3. New York: Bahá'í Publishing Committee, 1980.

[5] idem. *The Promulgation of Universal Peace*, 1982 edition. Wilmette: Bahá'í Publishing Trust, 1982.

[6] idem. *Some Answered Questions*. Bahá'í Publishing Trust, 1987.

[7] idem. *The Secret of Divine Civilization*. Wilmette: Bahá'í Publishing Trust, 1990.

[8] idem. *Lights of Guidance: A Bahá'í Reference File*. India Bahá'í Publishing Trust, 1994. Compiled by Helen Hornby.

[9] idem. *Paris Talks*. Bahá'í Publishing Trust, 1995.

[10] Arnold, Matthew. "Stanzas from the Grande Chartreuse", in Miriam Allot and Robert H. Super, eds. *Matthew Arnold*. Oxford: Oxford University Press, 1986.

[11] Bahá'u'lláh. *Gleanings from the Writings of Bahá'u'lláh*. Bahá'í Publishing Trust, 1983.

[12] idem. *Ḥuqúqu'lláh: A Compilation*. National Spiritual Assembly of the Bahá'ís of Canada, 1986.

[13] idem. *Tablets of Bahá'u'lláh.* Wilmette: Bahá'í Publishing Trust, 1988.

[14] idem. *Tablets of Bahá'u'lláh Revealed After the Kitáb-i-Aqdas.* US Bahá'í Publishing Trust, 1988.

[15] idem. *Kitáb-i-Aqdas.* Bahá'í World Center, 1992.

[16] Benson, Bruce L. *The Enterprise of Law: Justice Without The State.* Pacific Research Institute for Public Policy, 1990.

[17] Burke, Edmund. "Reflections on the Revolution in France", in *The Works of the Right Honourable Edmund Burke.* Vol. 2. London: Henry G. Bohn, 1864.

[18] Capra, Fritjof. *The Turning Point.* New York: Simon and Schuster, 1984.

[19] Dickens, Charles. *A Tale of Two Cities.* New York: Dodd, Mead & Co. 1942.

[20] Effendi, Shoghi. *Bahá'í Administration.* US Bahá'í Publishing Trust, 1974.

[21] idem. *The World Order of Bahá'u'lláh: Selected Letters by Shoghi Effendi.* Bahá'í Publishing Trust, 1982.

[22] idem. *The Advent of Divine Justice.* Bahá'í Publishing Trust, 1990.

[23] Fuller, Lon L. *The Principles of Social Order,* revised edition. Hart Publishing, 2002.

[24] Gibran, Kahlil. *The Prophet.* Oxford: Oneworld Publications, 1995.

[25] Greaves, Bettina Bien, ed. *Austrian Economics: An Anthology.* Irvington-on-Hudson, NY: Foundation for Economic Education, 1996.

[26] Hazlitt, Henry. *The Foundations of Morality.* New York: The Foundation for Economic Education, 1998.

[27] idem. *Thinking as a Science.* Ludwig von Mises Institute, 2008.

[28] Howard, Philip K. *The Lost Art of Drawing the Line.* New York: Random House, 2001.

[29] Huerta de Soto, Jesús. *Money, Bank Credit, and Economic Cycles.* Ludwig von Mises Institute, 2009.

[30] Hülsmann, Jörg Guido. *Mises: The Last Knight of Liberalism.* Auburn: Ludwig von Mises Institute, 2007.

[31] idem. *The Ethics of Money Production.* Ludwig von Mises Institute, 2008.

[32] Kinsella, Stephan. "Knowledge is Power". Mises Blog, December 28 2010.
URL: http://blog.mises.org/15149/knowledge-is-power/.

[33] Koerber, Bruce. *More Than Laissez-Faire.* Vol. 1 of *Divine Economy.* Manitoba: Invisible Order, 2015, ISBN 978-0-9960955-5-6.
URL: http://www.divineeconomytheory.com/books/ more-than-laissez-faire.

[34] idem. *The Human Essence of Economics.* Vol. 2 of *Divine Economy.* Manitoba: Invisible Order, 2015, ISBN 978-0-9960955-6-3.
URL: http://www.divineeconomytheory.com/books/ the-human-essence-of-economics.

[35] idem. *Ethical Economics for Today and Tomorrow.* Vol. 3 of *Divine Economy.* Manitoba: Invisible Order, 2015, ISBN 978-0-9960955-9-4.
URL: http://www.divineeconomytheory.com/books/ ethical-economics-for-today-and-tomorrow.

[36] Lample, Paul. *Revelation & Social Reality: Learning to Translate What Is Written into Reality.* Palabra Publications, 2009.

[37] Leoni, Bruno. *Freedom and the Law,* expanded third edition. Liberty Fund, 1991.

[38] "Luke 20:25" in Bible. *The Holy Bible.* King James Version.

[39] "Matthew 7:20" in Bible. *The Holy Bible.* King James Version.

[40] Mises, Ludwig von. *The Theory of Money and Credit.* Yale University Press, 1953.

[41] idem. *The Ultimate Foundation of Economic Science.* D. Van Nostrand Company, Inc. 1962.

[42] idem. *Planning for Freedom and twelve other essays and addresses,* memorial edition. Libertarian Press, 1974.

[43] idem. *A Critique of Interventionism,* reprint edition. Arlington House, 1977.

[44] idem. *Bureaucracy.* Center For Futures Education, 1983.

[45] idem. *Theory and History: An Interpretation of Social and Economic Evolution.* The Ludwig von Mises Institute, 1985.

[46] idem. *Liberalism in the Classical Tradition,* third edition. The Foundation for Economic Education, Inc., *and* Cobden Press, 1985.

[47] idem. *Money, Method and the Market Process.* Kluwer Academic Publishers, 1990.

[48] idem. *Human Action,* fourth edition. Irvington-on-Hudson, NY: Foundation for Economic Education, 1996.

[49] idem. *Epistemological Problems of Economics,* third edition. The Ludwig von Mises Institute, 2003.

[50] idem. *Economic Policy: Thoughts for Today and Tomorrow,* third edition. Ludwig von Mises Institute, 2006.

[51] idem. *Omnipotent Government: The Rise of the Total State and Total War.* Liberty Fund, *and* Ludwig von Mises Institute, 2010.

[52] Nisbet, Robert. *Prejudices: A Philosophical Dictionary.* Cambridge, Mass.: Harvard University Press, 1982.

[53] Reisman, George. "Globalization: The Long-Run Big Picture". Mises Daily, November 18 2006.
URL: http://mises.org/daily/2361/.

[54] Rothbard, Murray N. *For A New Liberty: The Libertarian Manifesto,* second edition. Ludwig von Mises Institute, 2006.

[55] idem. *Economic Thought Before Adam Smith.* Vol. 1 of *An Austrian Perspective on the History of Economic Thought.* Ludwig von Mises Institute, 2006.

[56] Stolyarov, G., II. "Ten Principles of Classical Liberalism: Fundamental Ideas in a Philosophy of Liberty". Rational Argumentator, July 2014.
URL: http://www.rationalargumentator.com/index/blog/2014/07/principles-classical-liberalism/.

[57] Universal House of Justice, The. *Messages on Behalf of the Universal House of Justice: 1963–1986.* US Bahá'í Publishing Trust, 1986. Compiled by Geoffry W. Marks.

About the Author

Bruce Koerber—the originator of the divine economy theory and the divine economy models.

The whole theory and the associated models developed as part of a deductive process. The simple model appeared to be organic and easily took on the characteristics inherent in the philosophy of classical liberalism. The first stage of its development ended with a dynamic macroeconomic model. Pursuing further the deductive process the model fit perfectly into a structural analysis that penetrated into the very heart of economic activity all the way to the origin of where value comes from. This discovery process yielded the microeconomic model.

Two major realms of the divine economy model remained unexplored. The first was the ethical strand which had to do with the connection between the human spirit expressed as purposeful human action, and transformation which is manifest in the capital structure. The perspective of the divine economy theory renewed macro and micro economics, granted, but the melding together of ethics and economics in theory and in a model had never been achieved before.

The last component of the divine economy model is just as earthshaking. This time the relationship between law and order brought to light the role of the equilibrium forces of the economy in the advancement of civilization by balancing all aspects of social cooperation, most notably liberty and justice.